Globe Fearon

Writing
IN THE
REAL WORLD

Globe
Fearon

Upper Saddle River, New Jersey
www.globefearon.com

Reviewers:

Pattye Clark
Secondary English Teacher
Pine Bluff High School
Pine Bluff, AR

Angelina M. Estes
Special Ed. Teacher
Pearland High School
Pearland, TX

Paul R. Gallaher
Department of Education
State of Florida
Tallahassee, FL

Natalie Mansbach
Educational Evaluator
District #26–Queens & M.S. 74
New York, NY

Diane Robertson
Resource Specialist
Twin Peaks Middle School
Poway, CA

Judi White
Head Teacher
Youth Consultation Service
Fort Lee, NJ

Executive Editor: Deborah Brennan
Project Editor: Kim Choi
Senior Editor: Lynn Kloss
Writer: Duncan Searl
Production Editor: Marcy Maslanczuk
Cover and Interior Design: Sharon Scannell
Electronic Page Production: Jeffrey Engel

Printed in the United States of America   4 5 6 7 8 9 10   04 03 02 01

ISBN: 0-130-23452-4

Globe
Fearon

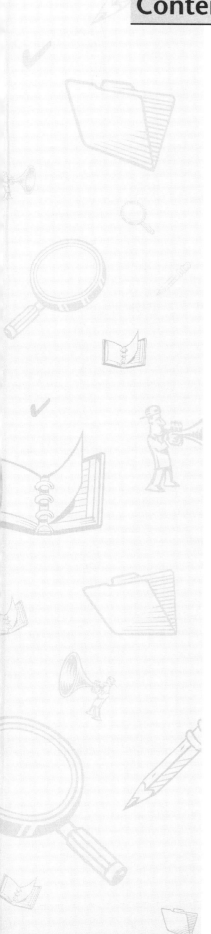

Contents

To the Student

You write in school every day. Writing is part of the real world too. When you begin to live on your own, you will need to write in everyday situations. This book will help you with "real world" writing.

Each unit in this book shows an area of life in which writing is important. You know that writing is important at school, but writing will help you at home and with your family and friends too. Writing is also part of community life. It plays a role in shopping and handling money. Finally, no matter what job you have, writing will be part of your work.

Each lesson in this book will help you learn about one type of writing. First there is a **Learn It** section. It explains what you need to know. The **Look At It** section shows you an example of a type of writing.

Next comes a **Talk About It** section. This is a chance to discuss the writing with some classmates. In the **Try It** section, you can try your hand at a writing task. Finally, the **Use It** activity lets you create a piece of writing on your own.

The writing you will do in this book is practical and important. You will make lists and schedules. You will practice filling out forms. These are real-life forms—the forms you fill out to get a driver's license, a credit card, or an apartment. Finally, you will learn about different types of letters and when you need to write them. As you work through the lessons in this book, you will build the skills you need to write—and live—successfully in the real world.

Unit One

ORGANIZING YOURSELF

Some kinds of writing can help people get organized at home and school. For example, people write lists, daily schedules, and summaries. They also write telephone messages, E-mail messages, and directions. Knowing how to do these things makes life at school and home much easier.

In Unit One, you will learn how to organize yourself.

Chapter **1**   **At School**

Chapter **2**   **At Home**

What Do You Know?

With a group of classmates, talk about what you do to get organized. Write a list of some types of writing that help you get things done at home and at school. How many types of writing can you think of? Save your list to use later.

Chapter 1

At School

What to Do First

Sondra does not know what to do first.

She has to write a report for social studies. It is due next week. The report has to be about people who work to make her community better. Sondra is not sure where to begin.

Sondra's English class is putting on a play. A month ago, Sondra agreed to paint the scenery. She also has to get the props, which are objects the actors will use on stage. The play is a week from Friday. The actors need the scenery and props right away. She has to get to work on them.

Sondra also has a big math test next week. She needs to study for the test. She should meet with Mrs. Williams, her math teacher, to get extra help too.

Just thinking about the next two weeks makes Sondra nervous. How will she get everything done?

Think About It

Think about these questions and discuss them with a partner. Then share your ideas with the class.

- Have you ever been very busy? How did you get organized?

- How might Sondra organize all the work she needs to do?

Lesson 1 Lists

Learning Objective
To organize yourself by writing a list

Word to Know
list a series of words or names

 LEARN IT When you have things to remember, you can organize them in a **list**. Begin a list with a title. The title shows the purpose of the list. All the items in a list should be related in some way. For example, you might make a list of things you need to pack for a trip.

A list can be written down a page in a column. It also can be written across the page in a row. When you write a list in a row, put a comma after each item. That makes the list easier to read.

A list should include:

- a title
- a series of related items
- commas between items (only if they are in a row)

Think about lists you have made in the past. What sorts of things did you list? Why were the lists useful?

 **LOOK AT IT**   On Monday morning, Sondra talks about the play with Mrs. Kim, her English teacher. As they talk, Sondra lists the props the actors need.

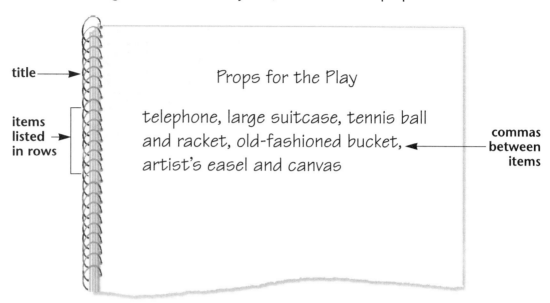

title →

items listed in rows →

Props for the Play

telephone, large suitcase, tennis ball and racket, old-fashioned bucket, artist's easel and canvas

commas between items

Sondra also could have listed the props in a column.

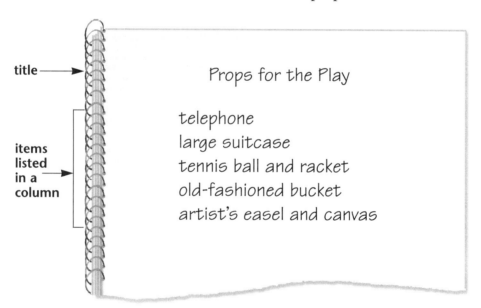

title →

items listed in a column →

Props for the Play

telephone
large suitcase
tennis ball and racket
old-fashioned bucket
artist's easel and canvas

 **TALK ABOUT IT**   How are the things in Sondra's list related? What title does she give to her list?

TRY IT

In art class, Sondra talks to Sharif and Kwan. The two of them agree to help her paint scenery for the play. Denise and Manny say they will help too. Manny says he can also get Zev and Becky to help.

In the space below, list the names of the students who will help Sondra paint scenery. List the names in a row. Remember to use the correct punctuation!

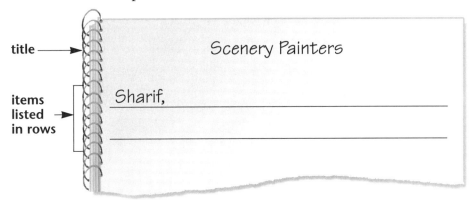

Now list the names of the students in a column.

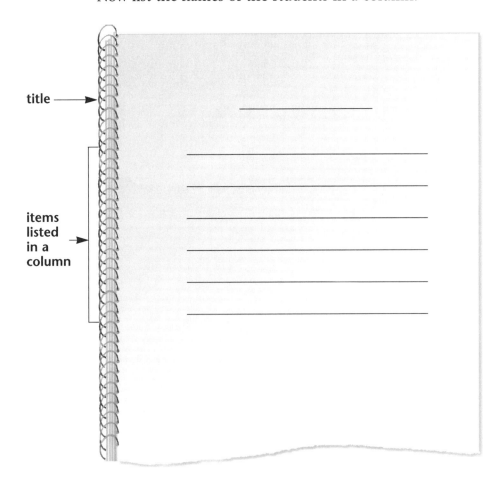

Use the Checklist to see if the list you wrote is clear and complete.

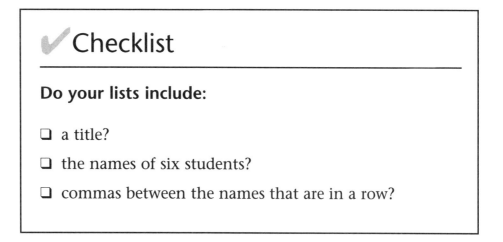

✔ Checklist

Do your lists include:

❑ a title?

❑ the names of six students?

❑ commas between the names that are in a row?

Did you leave anything out? If you did, add it to your list to make it complete.

 USE IT

Reminder

When you write a list in a row, put a comma after each item.

Suppose you had to write a report about workers who make your school a better place. You would probably begin by making a list of the five workers who make your school better. You can write the list in a row or in a column.

Write a draft of your list in the space below.

Use the Checklist to make sure your list is complete. Now write your final draft on a separate sheet of paper. Save your completed list in your portfolio.

Lesson 2 Daily Schedules

Learning Objective

To organize your time by creating a daily schedule

Words to Know

daily schedule a list of times for doing tasks each day

 LEARN IT

Getting organized means using your time well. A **daily schedule** will help you do that. Think of a daily schedule as a "Things to Do" list. It shows what you plan to do during a day. It also shows when you will do each thing.

At the top of your schedule, write the date or the day. On the left, list the hours that you have to do things. Next to each hour, list the task, or job, that you plan to do.

Think about how long it really takes to do each task. Give yourself enough time for each task. If you do not finish something on the schedule, you can add it to tomorrow's list.

A daily schedule should include:

- the date or day of the week

- the hours you can work on your tasks

- the task you plan to do each hour

Think about daily schedules. Have you ever made one? Why was it useful? If you made a daily schedule for today, what tasks would you list?

LOOK AT IT

Sondra has a busy two weeks ahead of her. She decides to make a daily schedule for each day. These schedules will help her make the best use of her time.

Here is Sondra's daily schedule for Tuesday. It shows how she plans to use her time after school and in the evening.

date or day →

hours Sondra can work on tasks →

tasks Sondra plans to do ←

TUESDAY

3:00–3:45	Go to Mrs. Williams's extra-help math class. Bring math problems.
4:00–4:30	Visit Community Action Center at 21 Main Street. Ask about community workers.
5:00–6:30	Sketch designs for play scenery.
6:30–7:30	Eat dinner, then relax. Talk to Mom about the props I need.
8:00–10:00	Study math and English.

TALK ABOUT IT

What things does Sondra plan to do before dinner on Tuesday? What things does she plan to do after dinner? Do you think Sondra allows enough time for each task? Explain your answer.

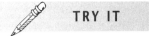

After school on Wednesday, Sondra has a lot to do. Between 3:00 and 3:30 P.M., she wants to show Mrs. Kim her sketches. Mrs. Kim will give her some suggestions. At 4:00 she plans to visit Ms. Green's office on Main Street. Ms. Green is a social worker and can give her some information for her report.

At 5:00, Sondra is going to visit her Uncle Ray. He has an easel and a tennis racket that Sondra can use for props. After dinner, around 6:30, Shawna is coming to Sondra's house. They plan to work on math together for about an hour. Sondra hopes to spend the rest of the evening studying science and social studies.

In the space below, make a daily schedule for what Sondra wants to do on Wednesday.

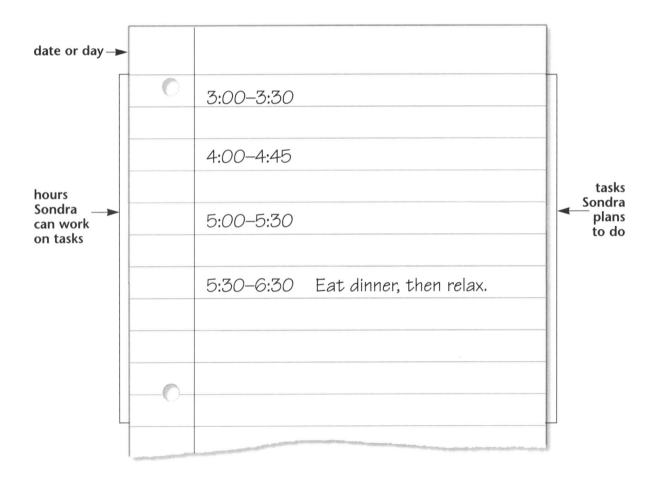

date or day →

hours Sondra can work on tasks →

tasks Sondra plans to do ←

3:00–3:30

4:00–4:45

5:00–5:30

5:30–6:30   Eat dinner, then relax.

Use the Checklist to see if the daily schedule you wrote is clear and complete.

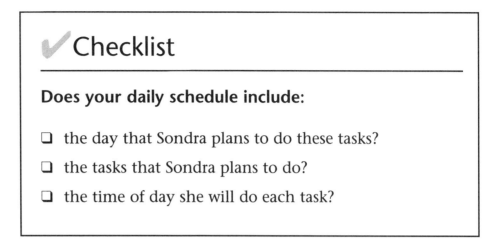

✔ Checklist

Does your daily schedule include:

❑ the day that Sondra plans to do these tasks?

❑ the tasks that Sondra plans to do?

❑ the time of day she will do each task?

Did you leave anything out? If you did, add it to Sondra's daily schedule to make it complete.

 USE IT

Think about your plans for this afternoon and evening. What are you planning to do? Make a daily schedule to help you organize your time.

Write a draft of your daily schedule in the space below.

Reminder

On your final draft, be sure to write your activities in time order.

Use the Checklist to make sure your schedule is complete. Now write your final draft on a separate sheet of paper. Save your daily schedule in your portfolio.

Lesson 3 Summaries

Learning Objective

To remember the most important points about a topic by writing a summary

Words to Know

summary a brief statement that gives the main points of an idea or topic

details small bits of information that add meaning but are less important than the main points

 LEARN IT

When you get organized, you must decide which things are most important and which are less important. One way to remember important ideas is to write a **summary**. A summary states the main points of a topic briefly. It leaves out less important **details**.

When you begin your summary, tell what the topic is. Then give important points about the topic. Your summary should answer some of the *Wh-* questions about your topic. The *Wh-* questions are *Who? What? When? Where?* and *Why?*

A summary should include:

- a topic sentence that tells what the summary is about
- the main points about the topic
- answers to at least some of the *Wh-* questions

Have you ever had to give a summary? Perhaps you tried to explain to a friend what happened on a TV show or in a book. Why are summaries useful?

On Thursday afternoon, Sondra visits the Community Action Center. While she is there, she talks with a social worker named Alice Green. Sondra is interested in finding out how Ms. Green's work makes her community a better place. Read Sondra's conversation below.

Sondra: How long have you worked at the Community Action Center, Ms. Green?

Alice Green: Oh, for about 18 years now.

Sondra: What do you like most about the job?

Alice Green: Well, it is always different and interesting! I get to help families with special needs.

Sondra: How do you help them?

Alice Green: I try to find homes for families who have lost theirs. Once I had to put a family in a motel for 2 months. I also arrange counseling for some children. Usually these children stay in foster care for a month or two.

Later, while working on her social studies report, Sondra writes a summary of her conversation with Ms. Green.

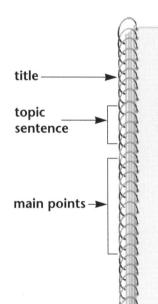

title ———→
topic sentence ———→
main points →

Summary of Meeting with Alice Green

Alice Green is a social worker at the Community Action Center. She makes our community a better place by helping families with special needs. Some of the ways she helps are by finding homes for the homeless, arranging counseling for children, and placing some children in foster care.

TALK ABOUT IT

Does Sondra's summary start by explaining what it is about? What *Wh-* questions does Sondra answer in her summary? What details has she left out? Tell why Sondra's summary is brief and clear.

TRY IT

After school on Friday, Sondra talks to Mrs. Kim about the scenery for the play. They talk about one of the scenes Sondra must paint. Here is their conversation:

Mrs. Kim: We'll need one panel, 12 feet by 8 feet. It has to show the beach and the ocean in the background.

Sondra: In the play, a storm is about to hit, right? The water should be dark with high waves. Should there be any boats?

Mrs. Kim: I think one sailboat racing for land would be okay.

Sondra: If a storm is coming, the beach should be empty, right?

Mrs. Kim: Right. You might have an overturned rowboat there. Add an empty lifeguard chair if you want.

Now write a summary of this conversation. Summarize what this scenery for the play should show. Be sure to answer some of the *Wh-* questions.

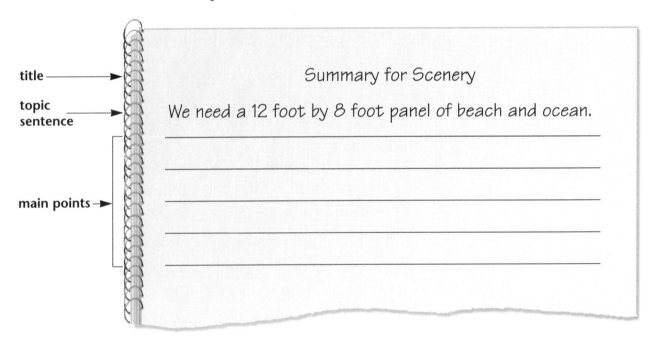

title →

topic sentence →

Summary for Scenery

We need a 12 foot by 8 foot panel of beach and ocean.

main points →

Use the Checklist to see if the summary you wrote is clear and complete.

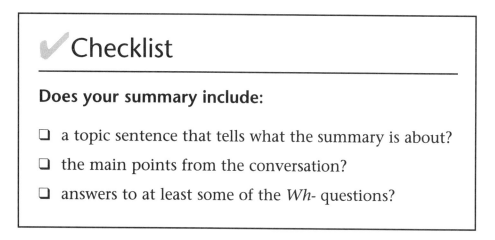

✔ Checklist

Does your summary include:

❑ a topic sentence that tells what the summary is about?

❑ the main points from the conversation?

❑ answers to at least some of the *Wh-* questions?

Did you leave out anything that is important? Did you include any details that were not really important? If so, go back to your summary. Make it brief and complete.

 USE IT

Sondra needs to paint one more scene. The scene will be set in the living room of a beach house. Read the description of the room in the play:

Scene 1: The living room of a 100-year-old beach house

The Johnson family loves the beach and spends every summer at this house. The living room is worn and has torn gray wallpaper. Through the two large open windows, we see sand dunes. Beyond the dunes is the sea.

In the background, we hear the ocean and seagulls calling. An old man sits in an easy chair in the center of the stage. He is staring at an old-fashioned clock on the wall between the windows.

Think about the description of the scene. What does Sondra need to know to paint the scene? Create a summary to help her remember the main points.

Write a draft of your summary on a separate sheet of paper. Use the Checklist to make sure your summary is complete. Now write your final draft on another sheet of paper. Save your summary in your portfolio.

Apply It in the Real World

Will Everything Get Done on Time?

Imagine that Sondra and three classmates are painting scenery for the play. As the days pass, she starts to get nervous. Will all the work get done on time?

Here are some of the problems Sondra will need to solve:

1. First, it is hard to remember how many paintings she needs and which ones are already done. One painting shows the beach during a storm. That one is almost done. Another painting shows a street fair. Then there is the inside of the Johnson's house. There might be another painting too—a scene showing a sailboat by the island—but she cannot really remember.

2. Sondra is not sure what is supposed to be in the street fair scene. Before she begins the scene, she wants to talk to Mrs. Kim. What would be a good way to briefly describe her ideas for the scene?

3. Another problem is when to do all the painting. Everyone in the group is busy with sports and studying. It is hard to find time to paint. The group has to organize its time. The group members need to know when they should be painting each day.

Decide and Write

A. As a group, talk about these problems. Tell the group what you think should be done. Decide which kinds of writing from Chapter 1 can help the painters get organized. How can each type of writing help the painters?

B. Have each group member create one type of writing you need. Use the information above and information from the chapter. Make up any other details that you need. When you finish, save your work in your portfolio.

Chapter 2

At Home

What a Week!

Devon had a very busy week. On Monday, his grandmother broke her hip. She had to go to the hospital. Relatives and friends called every day to find out how she was feeling. Devon took most of the messages.

Devon and his mother live near Grandma, so Devon's mother went to the hospital day and night. That meant Devon had to take care of things at home. His mother left him good directions.

Devon sent E-mail messages about Grandma's accident to relatives who live far away. Some of them came to see Grandma. They stayed at Devon's house.

On Friday, Grandma got out of the hospital. Then she had to stay at Devon's house for a few weeks. A group of relatives gathered to welcome her home. It was almost like a party.

It was a hard week. Luckily, Devon and his mother stayed organized and worked together. To keep a record of what happened, Devon wrote in his journal every day.

Think About It

Think about these questions and discuss them with a partner. Then share your ideas with the class.

- Do you take phone messages at home? Why are good messages important?

- Do you use E-mail? How does sending E-mail messages help you stay in touch with people?

- Have you ever written directions for how to do something? How did they help someone do a job easily?

- Do you ever write in a journal? How can writing about problems and feelings in a journal help you stay organized?

Lesson 1 Telephone Messages

Learning Objective

To remember phone calls for your family by writing telephone messages

Words to Know

telephone message a record of a phone call

 LEARN IT

Not every phone call is for you. Sometimes, you must take a **telephone message** for someone in your family. A telephone message can help families save time and money. Good messages also help families work together.

When you take a telephone message, make sure it is clear and complete. A good telephone message tells who called and the person's number. It also tells when and why the person called. Finally, it should tell who the message is for and who took the message.

A telephone message should include:

- the date and time of the call
- the name of the person who was called
- the name and number of the caller
- the message
- the name of the person who took the message

Think about some telephone messages you took at home recently. Were some messages unclear? Did some messages leave out important information?

Devon's phone rings at 4:30 on Monday afternoon. It is Aunt Sonia. This is the conversation he has with her.

Devon: Hello?

Aunt Sonia: Devon, this is Aunt Sonia. Is your mother home?

Devon: She'll be home soon.

Aunt Sonia: Grandma fell and broke her hip. She is at City Hospital in Room 312. I'm going there now.

Devon: Oh, no!

Aunt Sonia: Tell your mother to meet me there. Also, I need you to baby-sit B.J. for me. Can you hurry over?

Devon: Sure. Give me your phone number. I will leave a message for Mom.

Aunt Sonia: My number is 555-8686.

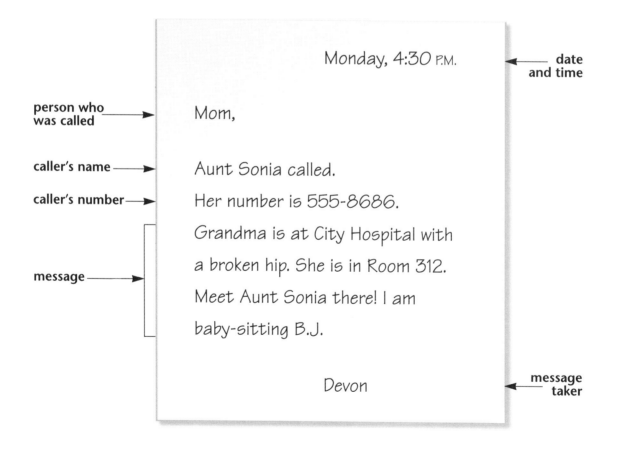

Monday, 4:30 P.M. ← date and time

person who was called →

Mom,

caller's name →

Aunt Sonia called.

caller's number →

Her number is 555-8686.

message →

Grandma is at City Hospital with a broken hip. She is in Room 312. Meet Aunt Sonia there! I am baby-sitting B.J.

Devon ← message taker

TALK ABOUT IT   What makes Devon's message clear and complete?

 **TRY IT**

Devon is baby-sitting B.J. at Aunt Sonia's house at 6:30 on Monday night. The phone rings and Devon answers. Read Devon's phone conversation.

Devon:	Hello?
Aunt Betty:	Hello, is Sonia there? This is her sister, Betty, in Chicago.
Devon:	Hi, Aunt Betty. This is Devon. Aunt Sonia's at the hospital. Did you hear about Grandma?
Aunt Betty:	Yes. I'm taking the train tonight. Tell Sonia to pick me up at the station at 8:30 A.M.—train number 4312.
Devon:	I'll leave a message. Give me your phone number in case she needs to call you back.
Aunt Betty:	Okay. It's 312-555-2943.

Imagine you are Devon. Write a telephone message for Aunt Sonia in the space below.

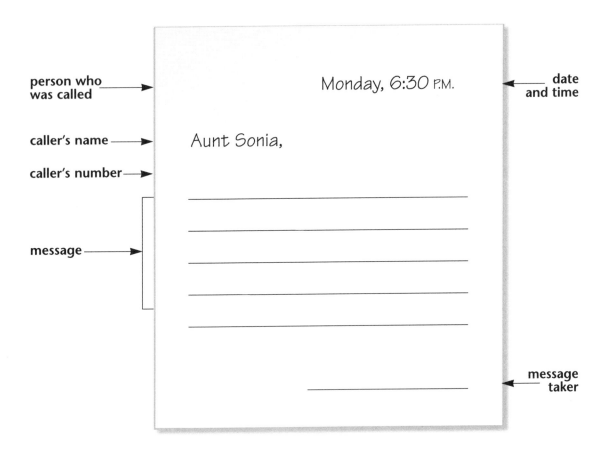

person who was called →

caller's name →

caller's number →

message →

Monday, 6:30 P.M. ← date and time

Aunt Sonia,

_____

_____

_____

_____

_____

_____ ← message taker

Use the Checklist to see if the telephone message you wrote is clear and complete.

✔ Checklist

Does your telephone message include:

- ❏ the date and time?
- ❏ who the message was for?
- ❏ the caller's name and number?
- ❏ a complete message?
- ❏ who took the message?

Did you leave anything out? If you did, add these items to your telephone message to make it complete.

 USE IT

Devon's mother is ready for work on Tuesday at 9:00 A.M. Just then the phone rings. It is Aunt Sonia. Her phone number is 555-8686. This is the phone conversation they have.

Aunt Sonia:	Grandma is doing well today. Tell Devon he can visit her at the hospital between 3:30 and 5:00 P.M. today.
Devon's Mother:	That's great! Devon has already left for school, but I'll leave him a message.

Pretend that you are Devon's mother. How can you get the message to Devon? Write a telephone message to let him know what is happening.

Prepare a draft of your message on a separate sheet of paper. Use the Checklist to make sure your message is complete.

Now write your final draft on another sheet of paper. Save your telephone message in your portfolio.

Lesson 2 E-mail Messages

Learning Objective
To send messages on the computer by using E-mail

Words to Know
E-mail address a group of letters that tells a computer where to send electronic mail

LEARN IT

More and more families use computers at home. People use computers to send and receive E-mail. A special computer program is used to write E-mail. In the *Send To* box, type the **E-mail address** of the person to whom you are writing. In the *Subject* box, type a few words that tell the subject of your message. In the *Message* box, type the message itself.

> ### An E-mail message should include:
>
> • the E-mail address of the person you are writing to
> • the subject of the E-mail message and the message

LOOK AT IT   Here is an E-mail message that Devon sent to his Uncle Joe.

E-mail address Devon is writing to ⟶

what E-mail is about ⟶

message ⟶

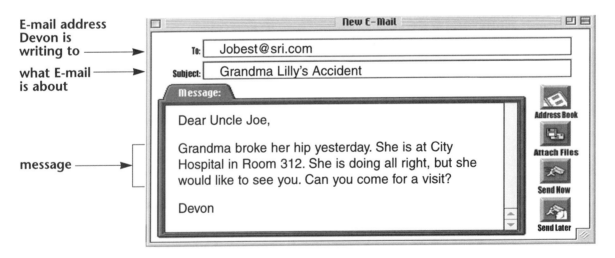

TALK ABOUT IT   Why is each part of an E-mail message important?

 **TRY IT**

Uncle Joe gets Devon's E-mail at work. He finds Devon's E-mail address—*Devtop@linkup.com*—and writes back. He writes that he and Aunt May will come on Wednesday. He wants Devon to ask his mother if they can stay at Devon's house for two days.

Write the E-mail message that Uncle Joe might have sent to Devon.

E-mail address Uncle Joe is writing to ⟶

what E-mail is about ⟶

message ⟶

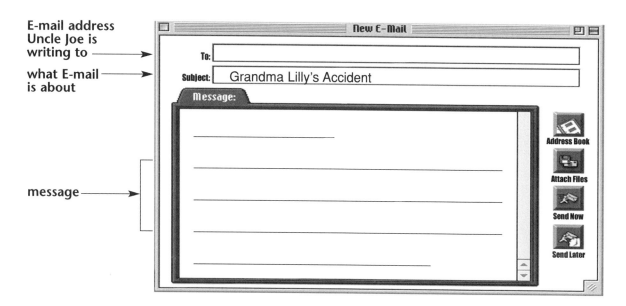

Use the Checklist to make sure your E-mail message is complete.

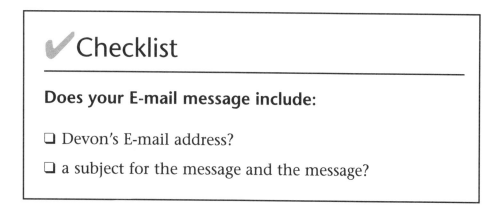

✔ Checklist

Does your E-mail message include:

❑ Devon's E-mail address?

❑ a subject for the message and the message?

 **USE IT**

Think of someone you would like to send a message to. Write an E-mail to that person about what is happening at home.

Prepare a draft of your E-mail message on a separate sheet of paper. Use the Checklist to make sure your message is complete.

Now write your final draft on the E-mail Message Form, which is Form 1A in *Forms in the Real World*. Save your E-mail message in your portfolio.

Lesson 3 Directions

Learning Objective
To help people follow steps by writing directions

Word to Know
directions a list of steps that tells how to do something

 LEARN IT

Directions help people do things. At home, you might write directions to tell someone how to fix or make something. You might leave directions for how to cook a meal. Good directions help people save time and energy.

Write directions as a list of steps. Always begin with the first step. Then write the rest of the steps in order. Each step should be clear and easy to follow. Be sure to use words that explain exactly what to do. Also, make sure you include every step. Leaving out a step will cause problems.

Directions should include:

- a title for the directions
- a list of numbered steps that are easy to follow
- steps that go in order from first to last
- all the steps needed to do something
- words that explain exactly what to do

Think about a time when you had to follow directions to make or do something. Were the directions easy to follow or were they hard? Why? What would have made the directions easier to use?

 **LOOK AT IT**

Devon's mother has been spending a lot of time at the hospital. Devon has been doing a lot of housework and making his own meals. On Tuesday, his mother leaves these directions for making macaroni and cheese.

title ⟶

exact words that tell what to do

list of numbered steps ⟶

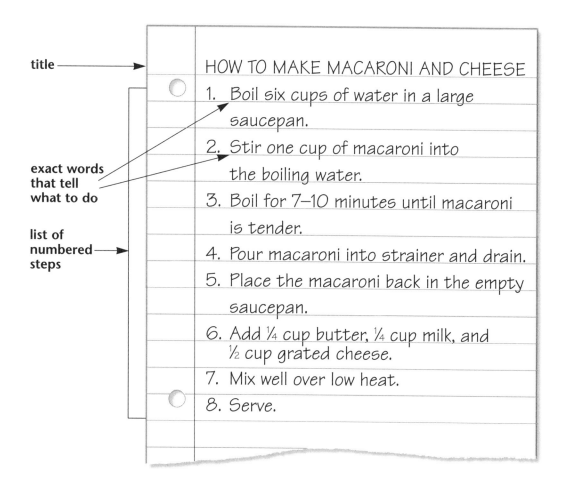

HOW TO MAKE MACARONI AND CHEESE
1. Boil six cups of water in a large saucepan.
2. Stir one cup of macaroni into the boiling water.
3. Boil for 7–10 minutes until macaroni is tender.
4. Pour macaroni into strainer and drain.
5. Place the macaroni back in the empty saucepan.
6. Add ¼ cup butter, ¼ cup milk, and ½ cup grated cheese.
7. Mix well over low heat.
8. Serve.

 **TALK ABOUT IT**

How many steps are in the directions? Are the steps in the correct order? What details make the directions clear and easy to follow?

TRY IT

Uncle Joe and Aunt May arrive at Devon's house. After visiting Grandma at the hospital, Devon and Uncle Joe go to the playground. Uncle Joe was a basketball star in college. Devon wants his uncle to work with him on his jump shots.

Read the conversation below. Uncle Joe is telling Devon how to make a jump shot.

Uncle Joe: To make a jump shot, start by facing the basket, feet flat on the ground.

Devon: Like this?

Uncle Joe: Bend your knees. Both feet must face the basket.

Devon: Okay. Now what?

Uncle Joe: Jump upward off both feet. As you jump, lift the ball past your face to a spot in front of your forehead.

Devon: This is as high as I can jump.

Uncle Joe: At the top of your jump, push your arms upward and release the ball with a strong flick of your wrists. Then follow the shot through with your arms and hands.

On the lines below, write directions for making a jump shot in basketball. Be sure to write your directions as a list of steps.

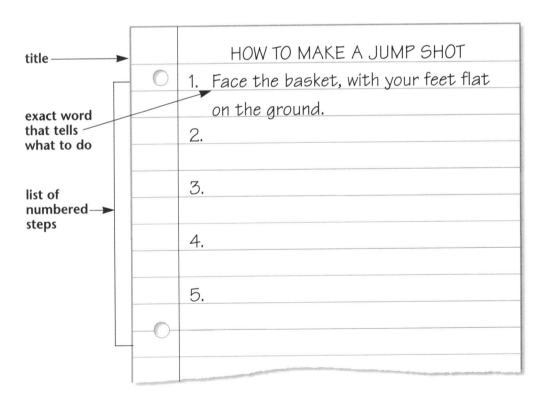

title ———————►

exact word that tells what to do

list of numbered steps ———►

HOW TO MAKE A JUMP SHOT

1. Face the basket, with your feet flat on the ground.

2.

3.

4.

5.

Use the Checklist to see if the directions you wrote are clear and easy to follow.

✔ Checklist

Do your directions include:

❑ a title for the directions?

❑ a list of numbered steps in the correct order?

❑ all the steps needed to make a jump shot?

❑ the exact words that tell someone what to do?

Did you leave anything out? If so, add it to your directions to make them complete.

 USE IT

From time to time, you will have to write directions for how to do something at your house. You might want to teach a friend how to play a game or make something. You might want a neighbor to water your plants or take care of a pet. You might want to give a brother or sister directions for cooking a meal.

Think about a job or activity that you know how to do. How can you explain to someone how to do it? Write directions with clear, numbered steps.

Prepare a draft of your directions in the space below.

Use the Checklist to make sure your directions are complete. Now write your final draft on a separate sheet of paper. Save your directions in your portfolio.

Lesson 4 Journal Entries

Learning Objective

To remember your thoughts about daily events by writing journal entries

Words to Know

journal a record of your personal experiences, thoughts, and feelings

entry what you write in your journal for one day

 LEARN IT

A **journal** is a good way to keep track of what happens each day. Start each **entry** in your journal with the date. That will help you remember when things happened.

Most people describe daily events in their journals. They might write about friends and family members. Journal entries might also include the writer's thoughts and feelings.

Some of your journal entries might tell about your hopes and plans. You could tell what you have done and still need to do. Used that way, a journal helps you organize yourself.

Journal entries are written from the "I," or "first-person," point of view. That means you use the words *I, me, mine,* and *our* to tell about what happened.

A journal entry should include:

- the date
- a description of events that happened
- your thoughts and feelings about these events

Have you ever kept a journal or diary? What sorts of things did you write about? How could a journal help you organize yourself?

It is a busy week at Devon's house. Devon's mother is spending a lot of time at the hospital. Uncle Joe and Aunt May are staying with Devon, and some other relatives are on their way. Devon is enjoying getting to know his uncle better.

On Thursday, Devon writes in his journal. He writes about some of the things that have happened. Notice that he also tells what he thinks and feels about these events.

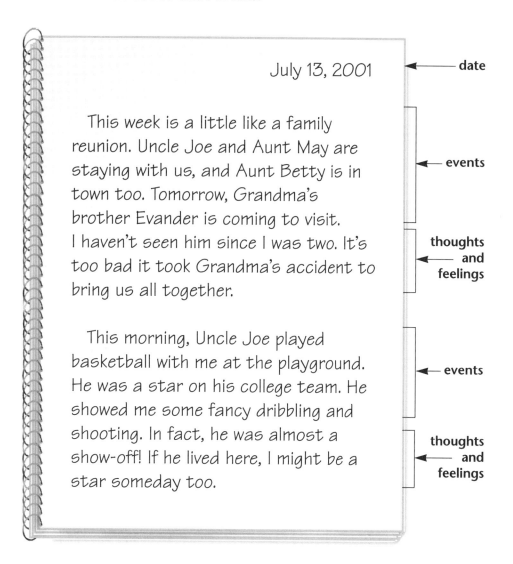

July 13, 2001 ← date

This week is a little like a family reunion. Uncle Joe and Aunt May are staying with us, and Aunt Betty is in town too. Tomorrow, Grandma's brother Evander is coming to visit. I haven't seen him since I was two. It's too bad it took Grandma's accident to bring us all together.

← events

← thoughts and feelings

This morning, Uncle Joe played basketball with me at the playground. He was a star on his college team. He showed me some fancy dribbling and shooting. In fact, he was almost a show-off! If he lived here, I might be a star someday too.

← events

← thoughts and feelings

**TALK ABOUT IT**

On what day does Devon write his journal entry? What events does he choose to write about? What thoughts and feelings does he include in his journal entry?

TRY IT

On Friday morning, Grandma's brother Evander arrives. Then Grandma comes home from the hospital in a special van. Two men carry her up in a wheelchair. Grandma is happy to see everyone. She looks tired though. Evander plays his guitar. He sings songs that Grandma liked years ago. That cheers everyone up.

Devon's mother makes hamburgers for lunch. After lunch, Uncle Joe and Aunt May plan to leave. Before they go, Uncle Joe invites Devon to visit them. After everyone leaves, Devon asks Grandma about growing up down South. Grandma says she could spend the next few weeks telling Devon the story of her life. Devon says he would like that. He might even write some stories about her.

Pretend you are Devon. Write his journal entry for Friday. The date is July 14. Tell about the events described above. Be sure to write from Devon's point of view. That is, use the words *I, me, mine,* and *our* to tell the events. Be sure to tell Devon's thoughts and feelings about what happened. Make up any details that you need.

⟵ date

Grandma's brother Evander arrived today. I really like him. Then Grandma finally came home in a special van.

events or
thoughts
⟵ and
feelings

Use the Checklist to see if the journal entry you wrote is clear and complete.

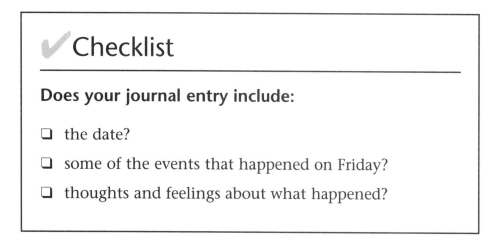

✔ Checklist

Does your journal entry include:

❑ the date?

❑ some of the events that happened on Friday?

❑ thoughts and feelings about what happened?

Are you happy with the journal entry you wrote? Is there anything you would like to add or change? If so, go back to your journal entry and make the changes.

 USE IT   Think about the events in your day today. How will you remember them for the future? Write a journal entry describing your day.

Prepare a draft of your journal entry in the space below.

Reminder

Begin a journal entry with the date.

Use the Checklist to make sure your entry is complete. Now write your final draft on a separate sheet of paper. Save your journal entry in your portfolio.

Chapter 2

Apply It in the Real World

Taking Care of Things at Home

Imagine that you are Devon. You like having Grandma at your house. However, you have lots of extra jobs to do for your family now.

Here are some things you need to do at home during the week:

1. Your mother asks you to make spaghetti one night. You do not know how to make spaghetti, but Grandma does. She tells you:
   "First, open the jar of sauce and pour it into a saucepan. Heat it over low heat. Then boil two quarts of water in a big pot. When the water boils, add the spaghetti. Cook the spaghetti for 8 minutes. Then pour the water and the spaghetti carefully into a strainer. Put the spaghetti into a serving dish. Finally, pour the sauce over the spaghetti and serve."
   What is the best way to remember what Grandma told you?

2. Uncle Joe has left. You keep having questions for him about basketball. Calling him on the phone is expensive though. Besides, you want him to write answers to your questions.

3. Dr. Halper's assistant calls when your mother is out. The doctor wants to change Grandma's appointment. Can Grandma come into the office next Wednesday at 2:00 P.M., not next Thursday at 4:00 P.M.? The assistant's phone number is 555-8776.

Decide and Write

A. In a group, talk about the jobs Devon has to do. Decide which type of writing from Chapter 2 will help Devon to stay organized. Discuss why each type of writing is important.

B. Divide up the writing jobs that need to be done. Have each group member create one of the types of writing you need, or use a form in *Forms in the Real World.* You can make up any details you need. When you finish, save your work in your portfolio.

WRAP-UP

In Unit One, you practiced seven different types of writing. Some of these types of writing will help you organize yourself at school. Others will help you get organized at home. The chart below lists the types of writing you have studied.

ORGANIZING YOURSELF

At School

- lists
- daily schedules
- summaries

At Home

- telephone messages
- E-mail messages
- directions
- journal entries

Read the types of writing on the chart above. Then choose two types of writing. On the lines below, describe a situation from your own life when you could have used each type of writing.

1. _____

   _____

2. _____

   _____

What Did You Learn?

On page 6, you made a list of writing tasks that you do at school and home. Look again at this list. Can you think of more items to add to the list? Add the types of writing you have practiced in this unit.

Unit Two

WRITING for FAMILY and FRIENDS

Some kinds of writing help you stay in touch with your family and friends. Cards, notes, and letters are good ways to share your feelings. You can write just to say hello or to share special events.

In Unit Two, you will learn how to stay in touch with family and friends.

Chapter **1**   **Expressing Personal Feelings**

Chapter **2**   **For Special Occasions**

What Do You Know?

Work with a group of classmates. Talk about the types of letters or notes you send to or receive from family and friends. List all the different types. Save your list to use later.

Expressing Personal Feelings

Missing Friends

Zina is spending most of the summer at the lake. Her whole family is there. The only problem is that Zina feels a little bored. She misses her friends. Because she is so far from home, it is too expensive to call them on the phone.

To keep in touch, Zina has been sending postcards to her friends. So far, she has sent out 23 postcards. Many of her friends have sent postcards back. That has been fun!

Zina has also been writing letters. Friendly letters are a good way to express ideas and feelings. Zina's friends have written letters back. As a result, they know each other better.

Zina also celebrated her birthday at the lake. A few relatives and friends sent her presents. Zina wrote thank-you notes to all of them.

The more cards and letters Zina sends, the more she gets. These days, the mail carrier brings Zina something almost every day. Writing certainly helps you keep in touch with those you care about when you are far away.

Think About It

Think about these questions and discuss them with a partner. Then share your ideas with the class.

- Do you send postcards to your friends when you are on a trip? Why?

- Do you know someone far away who would enjoy a friendly letter from you? What might you say in the letter?

- When was the last time you wrote a thank-you note? What did you thank the person for?

- Do you know how to write the addresses on an envelope?

Lesson 1 Postcards

Learning Objective
To send greetings by writing a postcard

Word to Know
postcard a small card used for sending a message by mail

 LEARN IT Postcards are a quick way to stay in touch with family and friends. People often write postcards when they travel. When you send a postcard, write the message on the left side. Begin with the date. Then write a greeting, such as *Dear Jack*. On the right side, write the name and the address of the person who will receive the postcard.

A postcard should include:

- a date, a greeting, a message, and a closing on the left
- a name and an address on the right

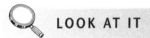 Look at the postcard that Zina sends to her best friend, Beebie.

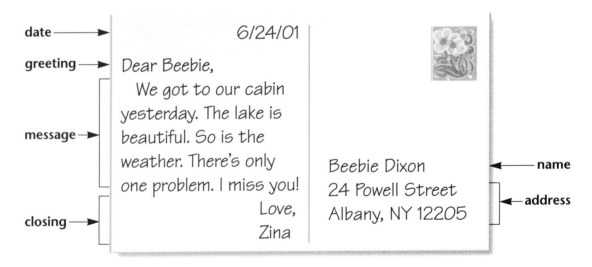

date → 6/24/01

greeting → Dear Beebie,

message → We got to our cabin yesterday. The lake is beautiful. So is the weather. There's only one problem. I miss you!

closing → Love, Zina

name ← Beebie Dixon

address ← 24 Powell Street Albany, NY 12205

 TALK ABOUT IT What does Zina say to her friend in the postcard?

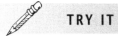

TRY IT

Pretend you are Zina. In the space below, write another postcard to Beebie. Invite her to visit you at the lake. Explain that your family likes this idea. Tell her that the week of July 1 would be ideal.

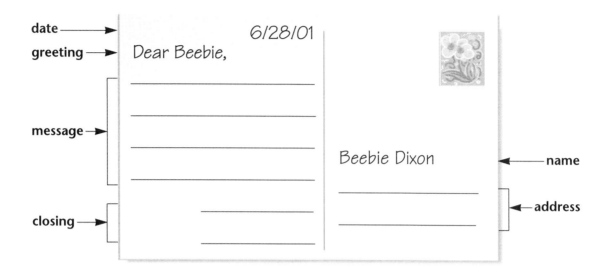

date →
greeting →

message →

closing →

6/28/01

Dear Beebie,

_____

_____

_____

_____

_____

Beebie Dixon

_____

_____

name ←

address ←

Use the Checklist to see if the postcard you wrote is clear and complete.

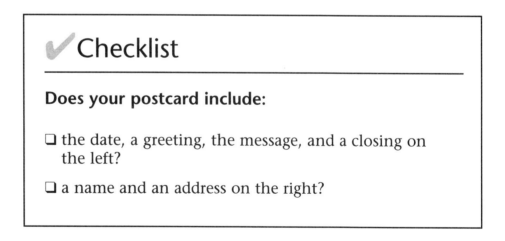

✔ Checklist

Does your postcard include:

❑ the date, a greeting, the message, and a closing on the left?

❑ a name and an address on the right?

USE IT

Imagine you are at the lake and you want to send a greeting to a friend. How will you do it? Write a postcard to let your friend know that you are thinking about him or her.

Prepare a draft of your postcard on a separate sheet of paper. Use the Checklist to make sure your postcard is complete.

Now write your final draft using Form 2A in *Forms in the Real World* or a real postcard. Save your postcard in your portfolio.

Lesson 2 | Thank-you Notes

Learning Objective

To say thank you by writing a note

Words to Know

thank-you note a short letter of thanks for a gift or favor

heading the date you write at the top of a letter

greeting the opening of a letter

 LEARN IT

A **thank-you note** shows that you are grateful. You should send a thank-you note to someone who gives you a gift. You should also send one to a person who does you a big favor. When you write, imagine you are talking to your friend or relative. Thank-you notes should sound friendly and personal.

You might buy blank thank-you cards at a store, or you might choose to write the note on a sheet of paper. Either way, the note should include the same information.

In a thank-you note, you should include a **heading** that states the date. You should also open a thank-you note with a **greeting** such as *Dear Aunt Sally*. Then tell what you are thanking the person for. Tell why you like the gift or why you are grateful. End your thank-you note with a closing such as *Yours truly* or *Love*. Then sign your name.

A thank-you note should include:

- a heading with the date
- a greeting
- what you are thanking the person for
- why you are grateful for the gift or favor
- a closing and your signed name

Think about thank-you notes you have sent or received. Why is it important to write thank-you notes?

LOOK AT IT

Zina invites Beebie to spend a week at the lake with her family. While Beebie is visiting, Zina's little brother Jon-Jon climbs into a canoe. A strong wind blows him out onto the lake. Beebie sees him just in time. Luckily, she is a strong swimmer. She races out to the canoe and pulls it to shore.

Beebie goes home the next day. Here is a thank-you note that Zina's mother sends to Beebie.

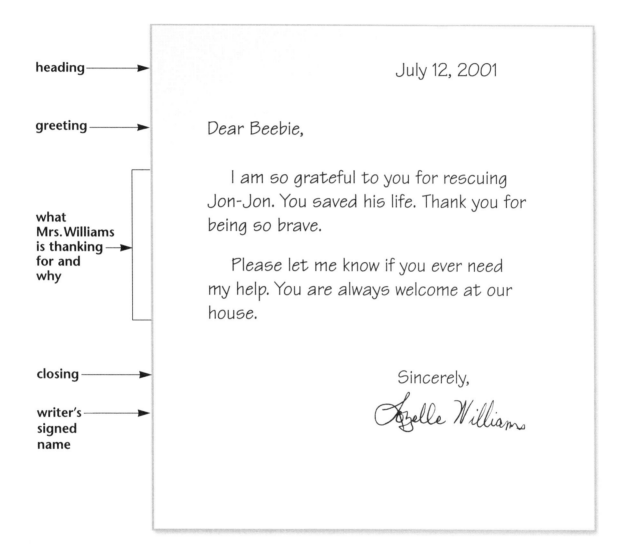

heading ——→ July 12, 2001

greeting ——→ Dear Beebie,

what Mrs. Williams is thanking for and why ——→ I am so grateful to you for rescuing Jon-Jon. You saved his life. Thank you for being so brave.

Please let me know if you ever need my help. You are always welcome at our house.

closing ——→ Sincerely,

writer's signed name ——→ *Lazelle Williams*

TALK ABOUT IT

Where does Mrs. Williams say what she is thanking Beebie for? How does she show that she is grateful?

TRY IT

Beebie writes a note to thank Mrs. Williams. She thanks Mrs. Williams for letting her visit. She says it was nice to get out of the city in the summer. She also says she enjoyed learning to sail.

In the space below, write Beebie's thank-you note. Use the ideas above. You may make up extra details if you like.

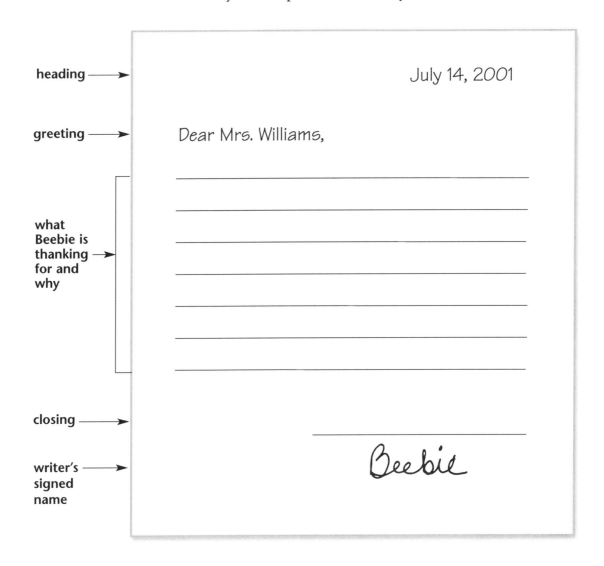

heading ⟶   July 14, 2001

greeting ⟶   Dear Mrs. Williams,

what Beebie is thanking for and why ⟶

closing ⟶

writer's signed name ⟶   *Beebie*

Use the Checklist to see if the thank-you note you wrote is clear and complete.

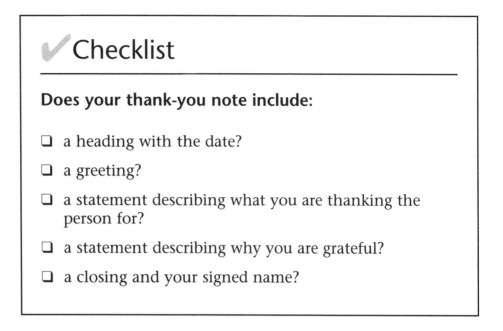

✔ Checklist

Does your thank-you note include:

❑ a heading with the date?

❑ a greeting?

❑ a statement describing what you are thanking the person for?

❑ a statement describing why you are grateful?

❑ a closing and your signed name?

Did you leave anything out? If you did, add it to your thank-you note to make it complete.

USE IT

Think about a gift or favor you may have received. How can you thank the person for his or her thoughtfulness? Write a thank-you note to let the person know how you feel. Prepare a draft of your note in the space below.

Use the Checklist to make sure your note is complete. Now write your final draft on a separate sheet of paper. Save your thank-you note in your portfolio.

Lesson 3 Friendly Letters

Learning Objective

To keep in touch with your friends and family by writing a letter

Words to Know

friendly letter a letter written to a friend or family member

body the main part or message of a letter

closing word(s) showing the end of a letter

 LEARN IT

Telephones and E-mail can help you stay in touch with your family and friends. However, you still need to write letters from time to time. **Friendly letters** are informal. They sound like two friends who are talking.

All friendly letters have the same five parts: heading, greeting, body, closing, and signature. Skip a space between each part of the letter. The heading is in the upper-right corner. It states the date. The greeting is the line that says, *Dear _____*. The greeting of a friendly letter ends with a comma. The **body** of the letter is your message.

In the body of a friendly letter, you share news and ideas. The **closing** signals the end of a letter. Use a closing that fits how well you know the person. Put a comma after the closing. The last part of a friendly letter is your signature, or your handwritten name.

A friendly letter should include:

- a heading with the date
- a greeting followed by a comma
- a body with news and ideas
- a closing followed by a comma
- the signature of the person who wrote the letter

Did you send a friendly letter to someone recently? To whom? What did you say in your letter?

As the summer passes, Zina writes letters to her friends at home. Her letters tell what she has been doing. By writing friendly letters, Zina stays in touch with the people she cares about.

Here is a friendly letter that Zina sends to her friend Beebie. Notice which parts of the letter begin with capital letters, where Zina writes each part of the letter, and where she uses commas.

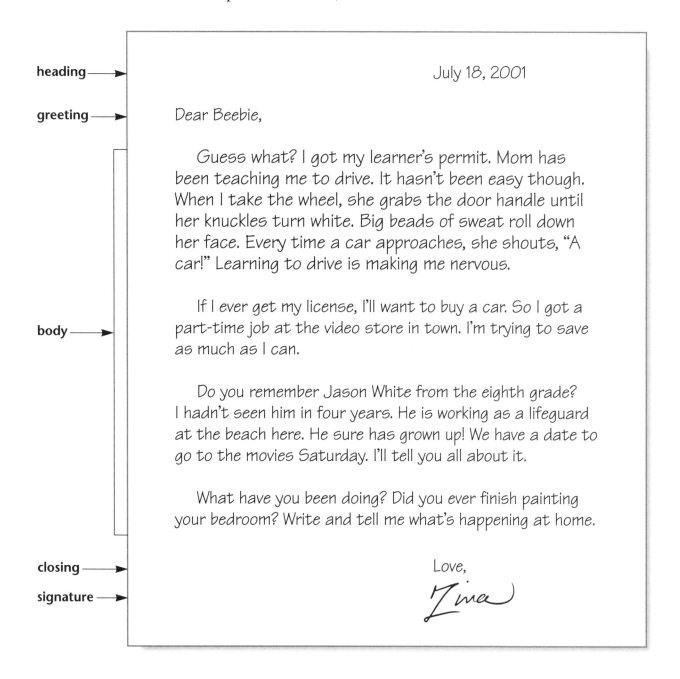

heading →

July 18, 2001

greeting →

Dear Beebie,

body →

Guess what? I got my learner's permit. Mom has been teaching me to drive. It hasn't been easy though. When I take the wheel, she grabs the door handle until her knuckles turn white. Big beads of sweat roll down her face. Every time a car approaches, she shouts, "A car!" Learning to drive is making me nervous.

If I ever get my license, I'll want to buy a car. So I got a part-time job at the video store in town. I'm trying to save as much as I can.

Do you remember Jason White from the eighth grade? I hadn't seen him in four years. He is working as a lifeguard at the beach here. He sure has grown up! We have a date to go to the movies Saturday. I'll tell you all about it.

What have you been doing? Did you ever finish painting your bedroom? Write and tell me what's happening at home.

closing →

Love,

signature →

Zina

TALK ABOUT IT

What news does Zina include in her letter? What words does she use for the greeting and the closing?

 **TRY IT**

Beebie answers Zina's letter on July 22. In her letter, Beebie tells how much she enjoyed Zina's description of learning to drive. She says she plans to take driver's education in school. She remembers Jason White. He played the trumpet off-key in the eighth-grade band.

Beebie says that she has a summer job too. She works at Pine Bush Park. She is on a team of teenagers that helps keep the park clean. The team members work on the nature trails too. Beebie says she likes learning about the environment.

Write Beebie's letter to Zina. Use the information above. You may make up other details if you wish.

heading ➤ _____

greeting ➤ Dear Zina,

_____
_____
_____
_____
_____

body ➤

_____
_____
_____
_____
_____
_____

closing ➤ _____

signature ➤ *Beebie*

Use the Checklist to see if the friendly letter you wrote is clear and complete.

✔ Checklist

Does your friendly letter include:

❑ a heading with the date?

❑ a greeting followed by a comma?

❑ a body with news and ideas?

❑ a closing followed by a comma?

❑ a signature?

Did you leave anything out? If you did, add it to your letter to make it complete.

USE IT

Think of a friend or relative you would like to write to. What will you tell him or her about? Write a friendly letter describing events in your life.

Prepare a draft of your letter in the space below.

Use the Checklist to make sure your letter is complete. Now write your final draft on a separate sheet of paper. Save your letter in your portfolio.

Lesson 4 **Envelopes**

Learning Objective
To write addresses on an envelope correctly

Words to Know
mailing address the address of the person receiving a letter
return address the address of the person sending a letter

 LEARN IT

Before mailing, you must write *two* addresses on an envelope. First, write the name and address of the person you are writing to. This is the **mailing address.** Write it in the center of the envelope. Then write your own name and address in the upper-left corner. This is the **return address.** Print or write the addresses neatly in ink.

An envelope should include:

- a mailing address
- a return address

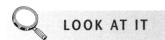 **LOOK AT IT**

Look at the addresses Zina wrote on her envelope. Notice that she used the abbreviation *NY* for *New York.*

return address →

Zina Williams
312 Lake Road
Greenfield, NY 13201

mailing address →

Ms. Beebie Dixon
24 Powell Street
Albany, NY 12205

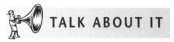 **TALK ABOUT IT**   Why must you write addresses on an envelope carefully? Why should you include your return address?

 TRY IT   Pretend you are Beebie. You write to Zina at her lake house. Fill out the envelope below correctly.

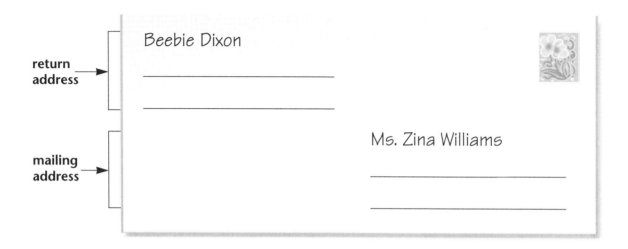

return
address →

Beebie Dixon

_____

_____

mailing
address →

Ms. Zina Williams

_____

_____

Use the Checklist to make sure you wrote the addresses on the envelope correctly.

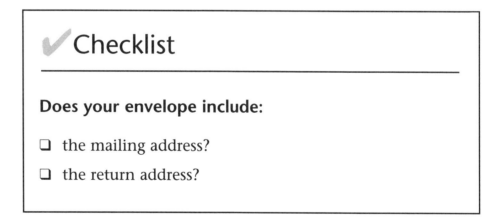

✔ Checklist

Does your envelope include:

❑ the mailing address?

❑ the return address?

 USE IT   Imagine you have just written a letter to a friend. Write the mailing address and the return address on an envelope. Use the Checklist to make sure your envelope is complete. When you finish, save your envelope in your portfolio.

Chapter 1

Apply It in the Real World

Keeping in Touch

Imagine that you are Zina. You are still at the lake. Summer is passing quickly. Still, you want to keep in touch with your family and friends. Here are some people you decide to write to:

1. You climb Snowy Mountain one morning. You remember climbing it long ago. Your Uncle Ron often took you hiking there. You decide to write to him. You want him to know that you are thinking of him.

2. Your friend Alex sends you a CD for your birthday. You want to tell him how much you like it.

3. In town, you run into Mr. Howell. He was a teacher who left your school three years ago. Mr. Howell tells you about his new work. He takes pictures underwater. He asks about your friend Beebie. Beebie thinks Mr. Howell is the best teacher she ever had. You decide to write to Beebie. You want to tell her about meeting Mr. Howell.

4. You send a letter to your cousin Terri. The post office returns it though. The envelope is stamped "Addressee unknown." You wrote Terri's old address by mistake. Her new address is Terri White, 1302 Corbett Street, Woodside, Delaware 19980.

Decide and Write

A. In a small group, discuss each of the people Zina wants to write to. Decide which type of writing from Chapter 1 will help Zina say what she wants to say. Think about what you have learned about each type of writing.

B. Have each group member create one of the types of writing you need. Use a form in *Forms in the Real World* if you choose. Use the Checklists in this chapter to check your work. When you finish, save your writing in your portfolio.

For Special Occasions

Busy Days

The end of June is a busy time. That is what Jan found out this year. She is graduating from high school. Already, she has received invitations to four graduation parties. Some of her friends are also planning a surprise party for her.

Changes are coming to all of her friends. Some of Jan's classmates are joining the army or navy. Others are leaving home for jobs or school. One is getting married. Jan sends letters to her friends on these special occasions. Jan also receives letters and presents in the mail. Her family and friends remember her special day.

In the middle of the excitement, there is bad news. While driving to her graduation from another state, Jan's father has a car accident. Jan writes to him in the hospital. She also plans to visit him at his home in another state. Jan can't stay long though. Her mother's fortieth birthday is coming up. Jan is planning a special dinner party.

July can be a busy month too!

Think About It

Think about these questions and discuss them with a partner. Then share your ideas with the class.

- Do you send written invitations to friends when you have a special party? Why?

- Why is it important to send replies to the invitations you receive?

- When something good happens to you, do you like people to take notice? What are some ways that friends do this?

- From time to time, friends and relatives face trouble and pain. How can writing a letter help?

Lesson 1 Invitations

Learning Objective

To ask someone to come to an event by writing an invitation

Words to Know

invitation a note or letter that invites someone to an event

RSVP an abbreviation that means "please respond"

LEARN IT

An **invitation** is a special kind of a friendly letter. It asks someone to come to an event. An invitation has the same five parts as a friendly letter. The body of an invitation gives important details. It tells the date and time of the event. It also tells where the event will take place.

When you write invitations, put yourself in the reader's place. Think about what he or she should know. For example, you might tell what the person should bring or wear.

The abbreviation *RSVP* helps you plan an event. Those letters stand for "Please respond," in French. You can write *RSVP* on an invitation. Then people will tell you if they are coming.

Reminder

The five parts of a friendly letter are the heading, greeting, body, closing, and signature.

An invitation should include:

- the five parts of a friendly letter
- the date and time of the event
- where the event will take place
- any special information readers need to know
- the abbreviation *RSVP* if you want to know who can attend

Think about invitations you have received. Were they written in friendly-letter form? What other types of invitations do people send?

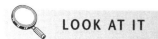

Jan Diaz is graduating from high school. Jan does not know it, but her friend Emma is planning a party for her.

Quentin receives this invitation in the mail. It tells him where and when Jan's party will take place. It also gives other information.

heading ⟶

greeting ⟶

body:
- date and time
- where event is
- special facts Quentin needs to know

closing ⟶

signature ⟶

RSVP ⟶

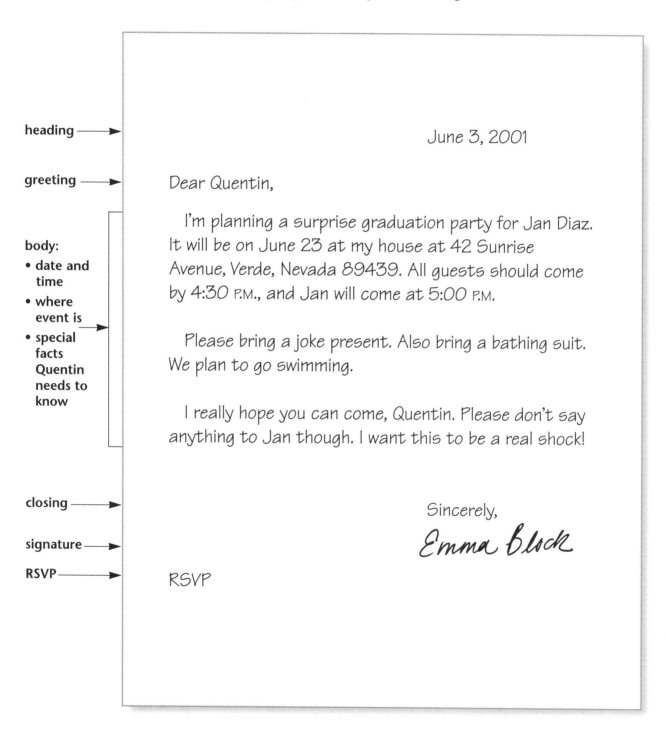

June 3, 2001

Dear Quentin,

I'm planning a surprise graduation party for Jan Diaz. It will be on June 23 at my house at 42 Sunrise Avenue, Verde, Nevada 89439. All guests should come by 4:30 P.M., and Jan will come at 5:00 P.M.

Please bring a joke present. Also bring a bathing suit. We plan to go swimming.

I really hope you can come, Quentin. Please don't say anything to Jan though. I want this to be a real shock!

Sincerely,

Emma Block

RSVP

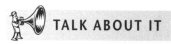

TALK ABOUT IT   What details about the party does Emma include in her invitation?

 **TRY IT**

Jan wants her stepbrother Corey to come to her graduation. Years ago, he used to help her with her homework. Now Corey does not visit very often. Jan misses him. So she decides to write a special invitation to him.

Write Jan's invitation to Corey. Jan's graduation is on June 30 at 8:00 P.M. The place is the Verde Civic Center at 1903 Center Street, Verde, Nevada. There are plenty of seats, so Corey will not need tickets. He can bring a friend. Jan is writing on June 3, 2001. Make up any other details that you need.

heading ⟶ _____

greeting ⟶ Dear Corey,

I really hope you can come to my graduation. _____

_____

_____

_____

body:
• date and time
• where event is
• special facts Corey needs to know

_____

_____

_____

_____

closing ⟶ Love,

signature ⟶ _____

Use the Checklist to see if the invitation you wrote is clear and complete.

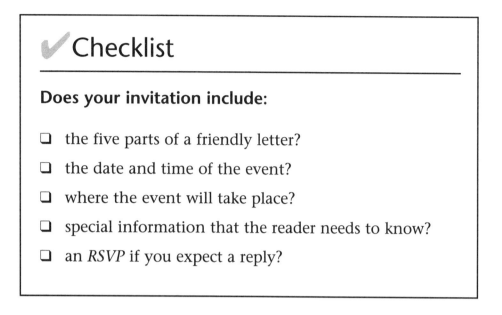

✔ Checklist

Does your invitation include:

❑ the five parts of a friendly letter?

❑ the date and time of the event?

❑ where the event will take place?

❑ special information that the reader needs to know?

❑ an *RSVP* if you expect a reply?

Are you happy with the invitation you wrote? Is there anything you would like to add or change? If so, go back and make the changes.

 USE IT Pretend that you are planning a party. Whom will you invite? Write an invitation that asks someone to come to your party.

Prepare a draft of your invitation in the space below.

Use the Checklist to make sure your invitation is complete. Now write your final draft on a separate sheet of paper. Save your invitation in your portfolio.

Lesson 2 Replies to Invitations

Learning Objective

To answer an invitation by replying to the sender

Word to Know

reply an answer to a letter or invitation

 LEARN IT

When you receive an invitation, send a **reply**. Tell if you can attend. Often, an invitation has a date next to the *RSVP*. You should send a reply by that date.

If you can attend, write a short reply. The reply should include all five parts of a friendly letter. In the body of the letter, thank the sender for the invitation. Say that you plan to come. State the date, time, and place of the event to make sure the facts are correct.

Sometimes you may not want to go to a party, or you may be busy. You should still send a reply. Again, thank the sender for the invitation. State the date, time, and place of the event. Explain why you cannot attend. Be careful not to write anything that will hurt the sender's feelings.

Reminder

The five parts of a friendly letter are the heading, greeting, body, closing, and signature.

A reply to an invitation should include:

- the five parts of a friendly letter
- a sentence thanking the sender for the invitation
- a sentence that tells if you plan to attend
- the date, time, and place of the event

Think about invitations you have received. Did you send replies to them? Have you ever wondered if people would attend a party you wanted to hold?

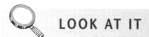

Quentin and Robert get invitations to Jan's surprise party. Read Quentin's reply below.

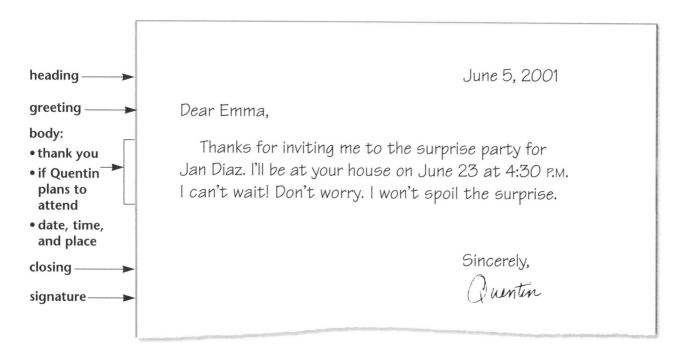

heading →

June 5, 2001

greeting →

Dear Emma,

body:
• thank you
• if Quentin plans to attend →
• date, time, and place

Thanks for inviting me to the surprise party for Jan Diaz. I'll be at your house on June 23 at 4:30 P.M. I can't wait! Don't worry. I won't spoil the surprise.

closing →

Sincerely,

signature →

Quentin

Read Robert's reply below.

heading →

June 5, 2001

greeting →

Dear Emma,

body:
• thank you
• if Robert plans to attend →
• date, time, and place

Thanks for inviting me to the party for Jan at 4:30 P.M. on June 23 at your house. I'm sorry I won't be able to come. My parents and I are going to a family reunion that weekend. I hope you have a good time.

closing →

Sincerely,

signature →

Robert

TALK ABOUT IT Who is going to the party? Who is not going? How are both replies similar?

Corey Rivera gets the invitation to Jan's graduation. The event is on June 30 at 8:00 P.M. The place is the Verde Civic Center, 1903 Center Street, Verde, Nevada. Corey is a sergeant in the army. He must go to a meeting that night. This means he cannot go to Jan's graduation.

Write Corey's reply to Jan's invitation. Tell why he cannot attend.

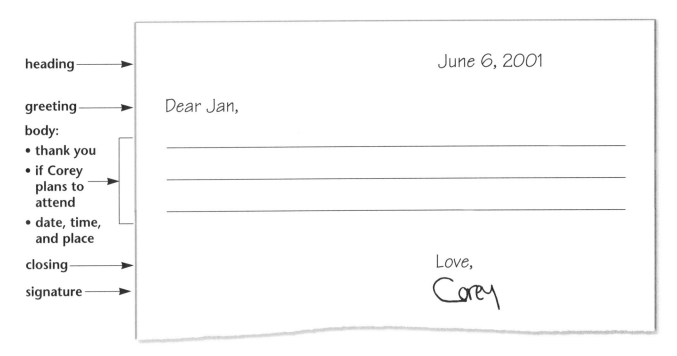

heading

June 6, 2001

greeting

Dear Jan,

body:
• thank you
• if Corey plans to attend
• date, time, and place

closing

Love,

signature

Corey

On June 10, Corey learns that his meeting has been canceled. Now he can go to Jan's graduation. Write another reply from Corey. Corey tells Jan that he plans to attend with a friend.

heading

greeting

Dear Jan,

body:
• thank you
• if Corey plans to attend
• date, time, and place

closing

signature

Corey

Use the Checklist to see if your replies to invitations are clear and complete.

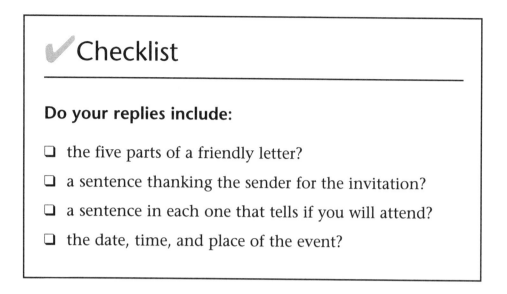

✔ Checklist

Do your replies include:

❑ the five parts of a friendly letter?

❑ a sentence thanking the sender for the invitation?

❑ a sentence in each one that tells if you will attend?

❑ the date, time, and place of the event?

Are you happy with your replies? Is there anything you would like to add or change? If so, go back and make the changes.

 USE IT Pretend you have been invited to a graduation party on July 1, 2001. What will you do? Write a reply to the invitation.

Prepare a draft of your reply in the space below.

Use the Checklist to make sure your reply is complete. Now write your final draft on a separate sheet of paper. Save your reply in your portfolio.

Lesson 3 Congratulatory Letters

Learning Objective
To congratulate someone by writing a letter

Words to Know
congratulatory letter a friendly letter that marks a special occasion in the life of a friend or relative

 LEARN IT

Often, relatives and friends have reasons to celebrate. They may have graduated from school. They may have gotten a job. They may have won a prize. **Congratulatory letters** mark these occasions. They show we are happy for others.

Begin a congratulatory letter by telling why you are writing. Tell why the occasion is important. Say why you are happy for the person.

Like a friendly letter, a congratulatory letter has five parts. It has a heading, a greeting, a body, a closing, and a signature. The words you choose depend on how well you know the person.

Write the letter soon after the special event. A friend may feel disappointed if you wait months to write. These letters are usually handwritten. That gives them a personal touch.

A congratulatory letter should include:

- the five parts of a friendly letter
- an opening that tells why you are sending congratulations
- why the special event is important
- why you are happy for the reader

Think about your family and friends. What good things have happened to them recently? Which events call for congratulations?

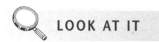 **LOOK AT IT**

Jan was not sure she was going to graduate. When she learned that she was, she told her relatives. Jan's grandmother wrote her this congratulatory letter.

heading ——————————▶

greeting ——————————▶

body:
• why Grandma is congratulating Jan
• why the event is important
• why Grandma is happy

closing ——————————▶

signature ——————————▶

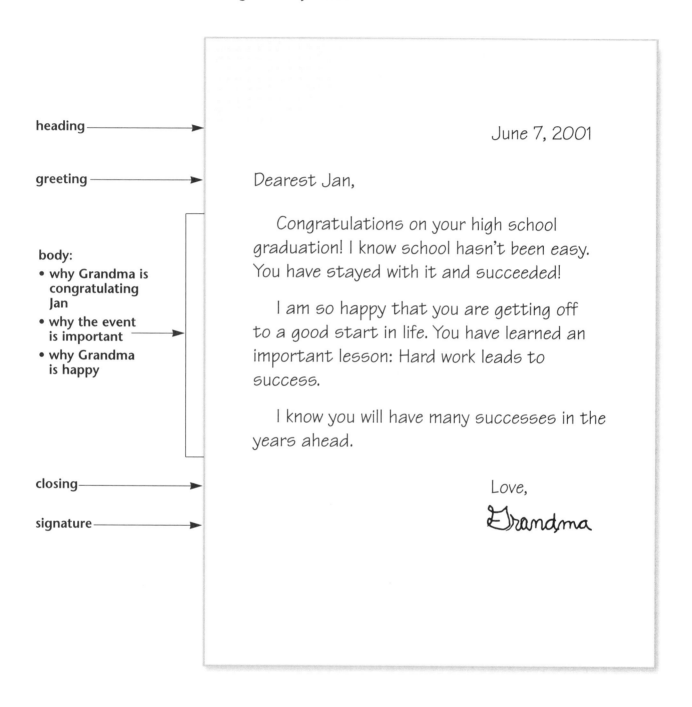

June 7, 2001

Dearest Jan,

Congratulations on your high school graduation! I know school hasn't been easy. You have stayed with it and succeeded!

I am so happy that you are getting off to a good start in life. You have learned an important lesson: Hard work leads to success.

I know you will have many successes in the years ahead.

Love,
Grandma

 **TALK ABOUT IT**

What greeting does Grandma use in her letter? Why does Grandma think the event is important? Why is she happy about it?

TRY IT

Jan's friend Robert has some good news. The navy has accepted him for computer training. By joining the navy, Robert will learn to work on computers. The navy will also pay him to take college classes later.

Jan is happy for Robert. She knows that Robert enjoys computers. She thinks this training will help him get a good job someday.

Write a congratulatory letter to Robert from Jan.

heading ———————▶   June 6, 2001

greeting ———————▶   Dear Robert,

        Congratulations on _____

_____

_____

body:
- why Jan is congratulating Robert ———▶
- why the event is important
- why Jan is happy

_____

_____

_____

_____

_____

closing ———————▶   Your friend,

signature ———————▶   Jan

Use the Checklist to see if your congratulatory letter is clear and complete.

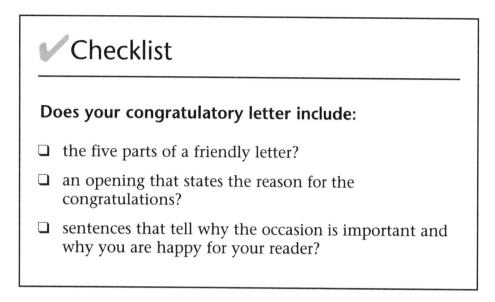

✔ Checklist

Does your congratulatory letter include:

❑ the five parts of a friendly letter?

❑ an opening that states the reason for the congratulations?

❑ sentences that tell why the occasion is important and why you are happy for your reader?

Are you happy with your letter? Is there anything you would like to add or change? If so, go back and make the changes.

 USE IT Think of a friend or relative who has something to celebrate. Write a congratulatory letter. How would you tell the person you are happy for him or her?

Prepare a draft for your congratulatory letter in the space below.

Use the Checklist to make sure your letter is complete. Now write your final draft on a separate sheet of paper. Save your congratulatory letter in your portfolio.

Lesson 4 Sympathy Letters

Learning Objective

To show your sympathy by writing a letter

Words to Know

sympathy letter a friendly letter that states your feelings about someone's accident or loss

 LEARN IT

Our relatives and friends sometimes face sadness. Death, illness, and other troubles are a part of life. A **sympathy letter** shows that you care. It shows you feel sorrow for your reader's pain. Like other friendly letters, a sympathy letter has five parts.

Putting sad thoughts into words is not easy. Begin by expressing your sorrow. State your feelings honestly. Let the person know you are thinking of him or her. If possible, offer your help.

If your reader is sick or hurt, tell the person to get well soon. Try to cheer the person up. Remember, however, that he or she is in pain. Be respectful. A sympathy letter should be warm and kind. It should be handwritten to make it more personal.

> **Reminder**
>
> The five parts of a friendly letter are the heading, greeting, body, closing, and signature.

A sympathy letter should include:

- the five parts of a friendly letter
- an opening that expresses the writer's sympathy
- an honest statement of the writer's feelings
- respectful words

Think about the times when your friends or relatives experienced bad times. What did you do to help?

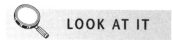

Jan's father is planning to come to Jan's graduation. He lives in California, more than 500 miles away. While driving to the graduation, he is in a car accident. His arm is broken. He also needs 40 stitches in his foot. Jan's father will be okay. However, he will have to spend four days in the hospital.

Jan hears about the accident the day after graduation. She writes this letter to her father.

heading ———————————▶

greeting ———————————▶

body:
• expresses sympathy
• tells how Jan feels
• is respectful

closing ———————————▶

signature ———————————▶

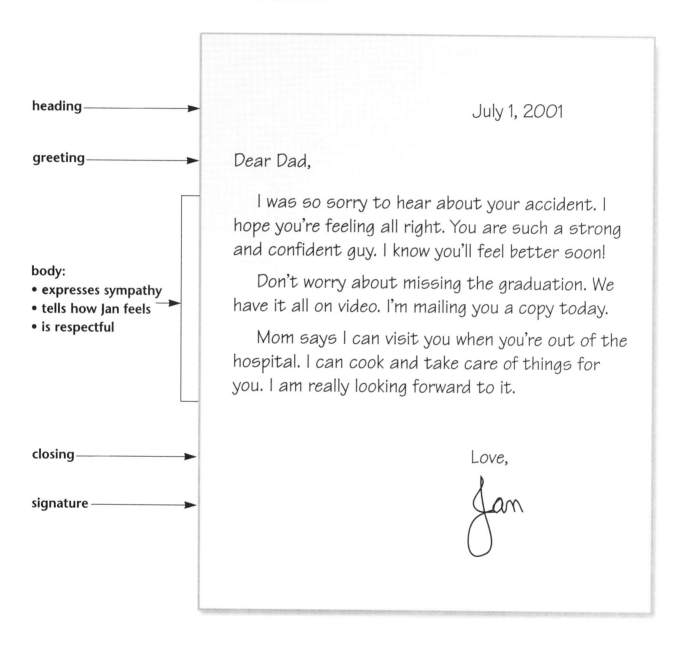

July 1, 2001

Dear Dad,

I was so sorry to hear about your accident. I hope you're feeling all right. You are such a strong and confident guy. I know you'll feel better soon!

Don't worry about missing the graduation. We have it all on video. I'm mailing you a copy today.

Mom says I can visit you when you're out of the hospital. I can cook and take care of things for you. I am really looking forward to it.

Love,

Jan

 **TALK ABOUT IT** How does Jan show her sympathy? What does she write to make her father feel better?

TRY IT

Jan's friend Robert is upset. He was planning to join the navy after graduation and was set to leave in August.

In early July, the navy gave Robert a physical exam. The doctor found that Robert has a heart murmur. It is not a serious problem, but it will keep Robert out of the navy.

Pretend you are Jan. Write a sympathy letter to Robert. Express your feelings about his disappointing news. Try to cheer Robert up. Point out that he might study computers at the community college. Say that you hope to spend time with him this summer.

heading ⟶ July 12, 2001

greeting ⟶ _____ ,

I am so sorry that you will not be joining the navy. _____

_____

_____

_____

_____

_____

_____

body:
• expresses sympathy
• tells how Jan feels
• is respectful

closing ⟶ _____

signature ⟶ *Jan*

Use the Checklist to see if your sympathy letter is clear and complete.

✔ Checklist

Does your sympathy letter include:

❏ the five parts of a friendly letter?

❏ an opening that states your sympathy?

❏ an honest statement of your feelings?

❏ respectful words?

Are you happy with your sympathy letter? Is there anything you would like to add or change? If so, go back and make the changes.

 USE IT

Think of a friend or relative who has suffered an illness, loss, or big disappointment. How will you express your feelings to him or her? Write a sympathy letter.

Prepare a draft of your sympathy letter in the space below.

Use the Checklist to make sure your letter is complete. Now write your final draft on a separate sheet of paper. Save your sympathy letter in your portfolio.

Chapter 2

Apply It in the Real World

News, Good and Bad

Jan is busy after graduation. Her friends and family have some special occasions. Jan writes letters for these special events.

Here are some events Jan needs letters for:

1. Jan's older sister, Carlotta, has some special news. She and her boyfriend Tom are engaged. They will get married next year. Jan is happy for them. She wants them to know how she feels.

2. Mr. Morelli was Jan's favorite teacher. His wife has just passed away after a long illness. Jan is thinking about Mr. Morelli. She wants him to know how sorry she is.

3. Jan receives an invitation to a party for her friend Eric. Eric's mother, Mrs. Ahn, is giving the party. The party is on July 5 at 8:00 P.M. at the Town Square Restaurant. Jan will not be able to go. She will be visiting her father in California that week.

4. Jan wants to give a small dinner party for her mother's birthday. The party is on August 7 at 7:00 P.M. at Jan's house. Jan's address is 211 Mesa Court, Verde, Nevada. Jan decides to invite Evelyn Rogers. Ms. Rogers worked with Jan's mother years ago.

Decide and Write

A. In a small group, discuss each special event. Decide which type of writing from Chapter 2 Jan needs for each one. Remember what you learned about each type.

B. Have each group member write one of the letters for Jan. Use the Checklists in this chapter to check your work. When you finish, save your work in your portfolio.

Unit Two

WRAP-UP

In Unit Two, you practiced writing different types of letters and notes. Some of these letters you could write any time. Others are for special occasions. All of the letters and notes, however, will help you keep in touch with family and friends.

WRITING for FAMILY and FRIENDS

Expressing Personal Feelings

- Postcards
- Thank-you Notes
- Friendly Letters
- Envelopes

For Special Occasions

- Invitations
- Replies to Invitations
- Congratulatory Letters
- Sympathy Letters

Read the types of writing on the chart. Then choose two types of writing. On the lines below, describe a time from your own life when you could have used each type.

1. _____

_____

2. _____

_____

What Did You Learn?

On page 38, you listed types of letters you send to or receive from family and friends. Look again at this list. Can you now think of more types of letters? Which ones should you add to your list?

Unit Three

WRITING for the COMMUNITY

Writing can help you take part in your community. You might write letters to find out what is going on. You might also write to express your views about the community. Having an apartment, getting mail, voting, and driving are also part of community life. To enjoy these things, you will need to fill out forms. In this unit, you will work on writing that helps you find your place in a community.

Here is what you will learn in Unit Three:

Chapter **1**   **Writing Letters**

Chapter **2**   **Completing Official Forms**

What Do You Know?

Work with a group of classmates. List community activities or programs you take part in now. Then list community activities you might like to take part in someday. Think about the types of writing you might do in each area. For example, are there any forms you will need to fill out? Save your lists to use later.

Writing Letters

Finding a Way

Jason Dietz uses a wheelchair. Last month, he moved to Village Falls. Now Jason is looking for activities. He wants to find out about wheelchair sports, for example.

Writing letters is a good way to find things out. Jason has been writing letters to places in his town. He asks for schedules of their activities.

Jason is unhappy when he receives the schedules. There are very few activities for people in wheelchairs. So he writes letters to point out that this is a problem. He wants the problem to be solved.

Jason wants people to know about this problem. Many people read the newspaper. So Jason writes letters to the editor. A letter to the editor is one way to speak out.

Jason is ready to take part in his community. He wants his community to welcome people in wheelchairs.

Think About It

Think about these questions and discuss them with a partner. Then share your ideas with the class.

- Have you ever written a letter to ask for something? What might you ask for in a letter?

- Why is it important to complain or speak out sometimes?

- Do you ever read letters to the editor in your local newspaper? What kinds of issues, or problems, do people write about?

Lesson 1 Letters of Inquiry

Learning Objective

To ask for something by writing a letter of inquiry

Words to Know

business letter a formal letter

inside address the name and address of a person who receives a business letter

letter of inquiry a business letter that asks the reader for something

 LEARN IT

Reminder

The five parts of a friendly letter are the heading, greeting, body, closing, and signature.

Friendly letters are personal and fun. **Business letters** are serious. When you write one, tell what you want in a few sentences. Be polite. Always type business letters.

Friendly letters have five parts. You learned about them in Unit Two, Chapter 1. Business letters have six parts. The sixth part is the **inside address**. The inside address is the name and address of the reader. Write it above the greeting. Use a colon (:) after the greeting. The heading should include the writer's address and the date. At the end of the letter, use a polite closing such as *Sincerely* or *Yours truly*.

A **letter of inquiry** is one type of business letter. It asks the reader to send you something or to do something for you. Tell exactly what you want. Give the reader enough information to help you.

A letter of inquiry should include:

- the six parts of a business letter
- a colon after the greeting
- what you are asking for
- all the facts the reader needs

Have you ever sent a letter to a group or business in your community? Did you receive the information you asked for?

LOOK AT IT

Jason uses a wheelchair to get around. He loves sports though. Right now, Jason would like to try some wheelchair sports. He writes letters to find out where he can play.

heading

inside
address

greeting

body:
• what Jason
  is asking for
• all the facts
  the reader
  needs

closing

signature

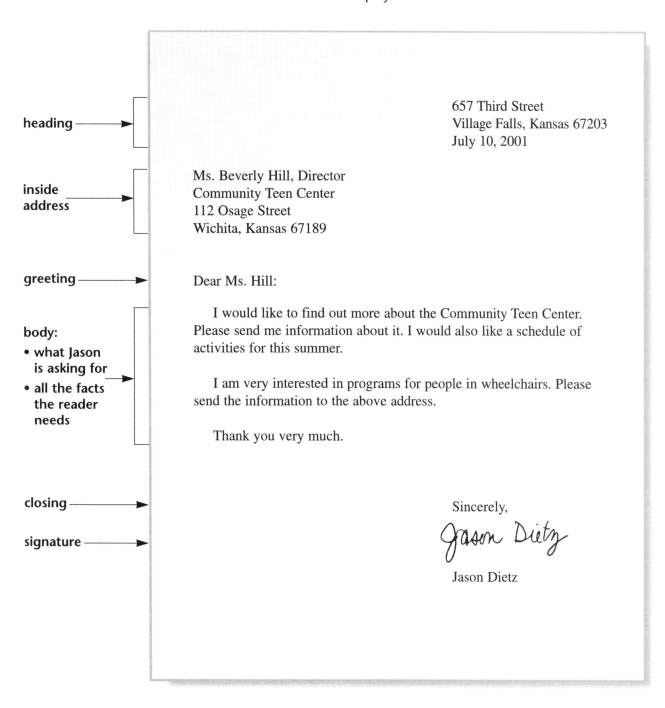

657 Third Street
Village Falls, Kansas 67203
July 10, 2001

Ms. Beverly Hill, Director
Community Teen Center
112 Osage Street
Wichita, Kansas 67189

Dear Ms. Hill:

I would like to find out more about the Community Teen Center. Please send me information about it. I would also like a schedule of activities for this summer.

I am very interested in programs for people in wheelchairs. Please send the information to the above address.

Thank you very much.

Sincerely,

Jason Dietz

Jason Dietz

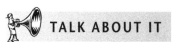

TALK ABOUT IT What information did Jason ask for? What fact about himself did he include to help his reader? Is Jason's letter polite?

TRY IT

Jason next writes to the Wichita Summer Recreation Program. Again, he wants information and a schedule. He asks about programs for teens in wheelchairs too.

Write Jason's letter of inquiry. The address he is writing to is 4000 Longview Road, Wichita, Kansas 67208. The person in charge is Mr. Don Lang. Jason writes on July 12, 2001.

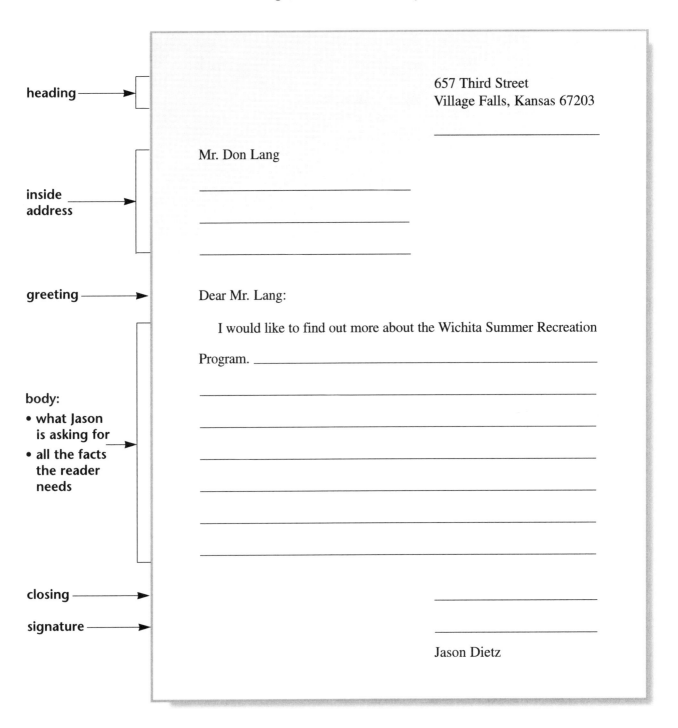

heading

657 Third Street
Village Falls, Kansas 67203

_____

inside address

Mr. Don Lang

_____

_____

_____

greeting

Dear Mr. Lang:

body:
• what Jason is asking for
• all the facts the reader needs

I would like to find out more about the Wichita Summer Recreation

Program. _____

_____

_____

_____

_____

_____

closing

_____

signature

_____

Jason Dietz

Use the Checklist to see if your letter of inquiry is clear and complete.

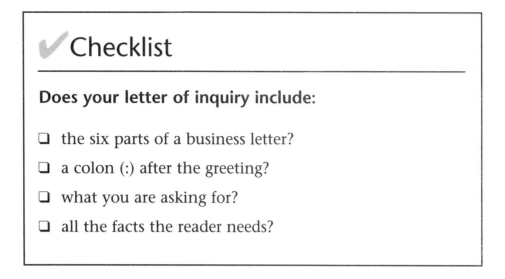

✔ Checklist

Does your letter of inquiry include:

❑ the six parts of a business letter?

❑ a colon (:) after the greeting?

❑ what you are asking for?

❑ all the facts the reader needs?

Are you happy with your letter? Is there anything you would like to add or change? If so, go back and make the changes.

 USE IT   Think about some information you would like to get from a group or business in your community. How will you get that information? Write a letter of inquiry.

Use the space below to make notes for your letter. You might note the items listed in the Checklist. Use your own address for the heading.

Write a draft of your letter on a separate sheet of paper. Type your final draft if you can. Save your letter of inquiry in your portfolio.

Lesson 2 Letters of Complaint

Learning Objective

To solve a problem by writing a letter of complaint

Words to Know

letter of complaint a business letter that asks someone
to solve a problem

LEARN IT

A **letter of complaint** is a type of business letter. It describes a problem. Then it suggests a way to solve it.

A letter of complaint should be brief and clear. Begin by naming the problem. The letter should say exactly what is wrong. Give the reader enough information to understand the problem. A letter of complaint should also suggest a way to solve the problem. That way the reader knows what to do.

Be polite when you write a letter of complaint. At the same time, be firm. After all, the problem must be solved.

A letter of complaint should include:

- the six parts of a business letter: the heading, inside address, greeting, body, closing, and signature

- what the problem is

- how to solve the problem

- polite yet firm language

Think about problems in your community. How could they be solved? Can you think of a person you could write to who can help solve these problems?

LOOK AT IT

A marathon is a 26-mile foot race. Many cities hold marathon races. Often, wheelchair athletes take part in them. Recently, Jason learned that Village Falls has a marathon. He also learned that wheelchair athletes could *not* enter. Jason writes a letter of complaint to point out that this is unfair.

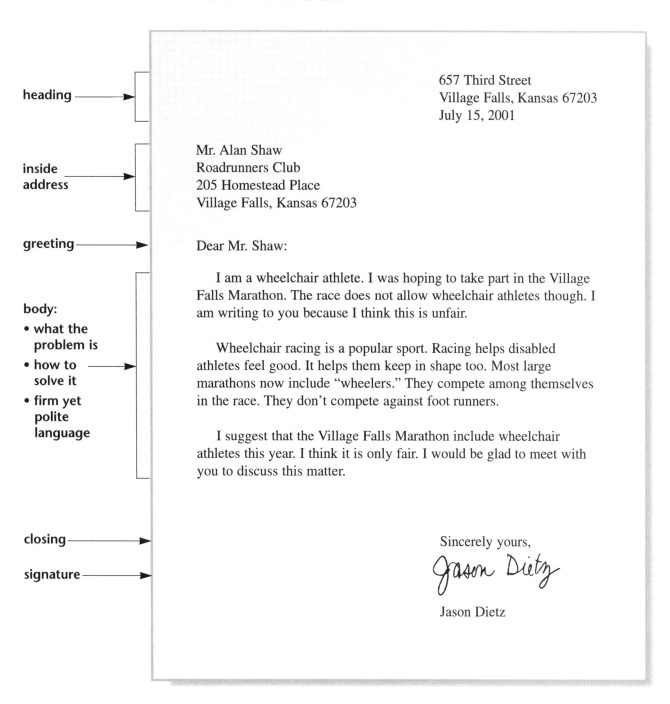

heading

657 Third Street
Village Falls, Kansas 67203
July 15, 2001

inside address

Mr. Alan Shaw
Roadrunners Club
205 Homestead Place
Village Falls, Kansas 67203

greeting

Dear Mr. Shaw:

body:
• what the problem is
• how to solve it
• firm yet polite language

    I am a wheelchair athlete. I was hoping to take part in the Village Falls Marathon. The race does not allow wheelchair athletes though. I am writing to you because I think this is unfair.

    Wheelchair racing is a popular sport. Racing helps disabled athletes feel good. It helps them keep in shape too. Most large marathons now include "wheelers." They compete among themselves in the race. They don't compete against foot runners.

    I suggest that the Village Falls Marathon include wheelchair athletes this year. I think it is only fair. I would be glad to meet with you to discuss this matter.

closing

Sincerely yours,

signature

Jason Dietz

Jason Dietz

TALK ABOUT IT

Where in the letter does Jason state the problem? What solution does he offer? What are some words that Jason uses to make his letter firm yet polite?

The high school in Village Falls has a pool. It is open to the public at night. Jason wants to swim there. Wheelchairs can fit through the main doors to the high school. At night, however, those doors are locked. The door to the pool is open. Five steps lead up to that door. In his wheelchair, Jason cannot use that door.

Jason writes to the school principal to complain about the door. He suggests that the main door be unlocked when the pool is open.

Write Jason's letter of complaint. Use today's date. Jason's address is 657 Third Street, Village Falls, Kansas 67203. The principal's name is Dr. Marian Davis. Her address is Village Falls High School, 250 Chestnut Street, Village Falls, Kansas 67203.

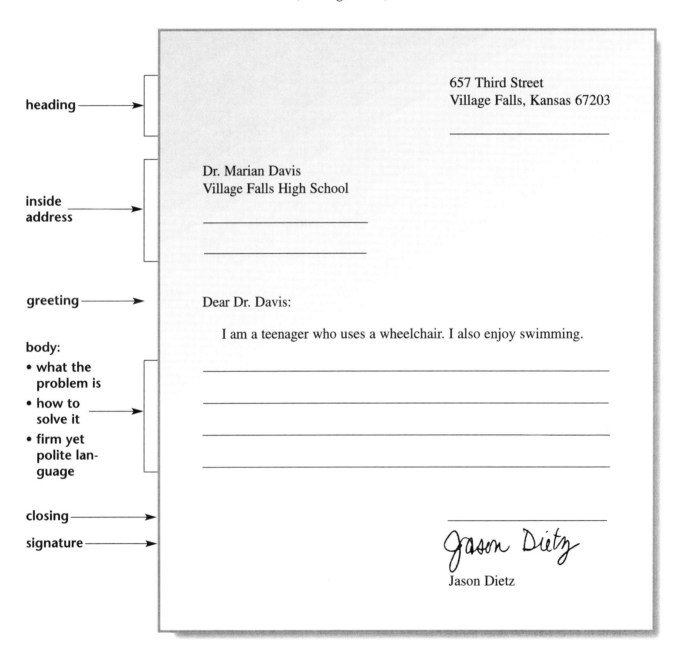

heading

657 Third Street
Village Falls, Kansas 67203
_____

inside address

Dr. Marian Davis
Village Falls High School

_____

_____

greeting

Dear Dr. Davis:

body:
• what the problem is
• how to solve it
• firm yet polite language

I am a teenager who uses a wheelchair. I also enjoy swimming.

_____

_____

_____

_____

closing

signature

_____

Jason Dietz

Jason Dietz

Use the Checklist to see if your letter of complaint is clear and complete.

✔ Checklist

Does your letter of complaint include:

- ❏ the six parts of a business letter?
- ❏ what Jason's problem is?
- ❏ how to solve the problem?
- ❏ polite yet firm language?

Are you satisfied with your letter? Is there anything you would like to change? If so, go back and make the changes.

 USE IT

Think of a problem in your school or community. Choose something that has caused you some trouble. How might the problem be solved? Write a letter of complaint.

Use the space below to make notes before you write your letter. You might note the items listed in the Checklist. Be sure to describe the problem. Then suggest how to solve it.

Write a draft of your letter on a separate sheet of paper. Type your final draft if you can. Save your letter of complaint in your portfolio.

Lesson 3 Letters to the Editor

Learning Objective

To share your ideas by writing a letter to the editor

Words to Know

letter to the editor a letter sent to an editor of a newspaper or magazine

opinion a statement of feelings or beliefs

 LEARN IT

Many people write letters to newspaper editors. They are called **letters to the editor**. These letters help people share their **opinions** with others. The letters are about important issues or problems. Editors print some letters in the newspaper every day. That way, readers learn about the issues. They find out why some people are in favor of an idea. They also find out why other people are against the same idea. War, taxes, and schools are common issues.

This type of letter states an opinion clearly. Then the writer supports the opinion with facts. The facts in the letter can help change newspaper readers' minds about the issue.

A letter to the editor is a business letter. It has an inside address. The greeting is *To the Editor*, followed by a colon (:).

Reminder

The six parts of a business letter are the heading, inside address, greeting, body, closing, and signature.

A letter to the editor should include:

- the six parts of a business letter
- the greeting *To the Editor,* followed by a colon (:)
- a clear opinion on an issue or problem
- facts that support the writer's opinion

What are some issues in your community that interest you? What opinion would you like others to know about?

The Independent Living Center wants to buy a house in Village Falls. Young disabled people would live at this center. They would learn how to live and work on their own. The mayor and town council do not like this plan. They say that the center does not belong in a family neighborhood. The town newspaper, the *Village Falls Herald-Times,* writes about the issue. When Jason reads the news story, he writes to the editor.

heading →

inside address →

greeting →

body:
• a clear opinion on the issue
• facts that support Jason's opinion

closing →

signature →

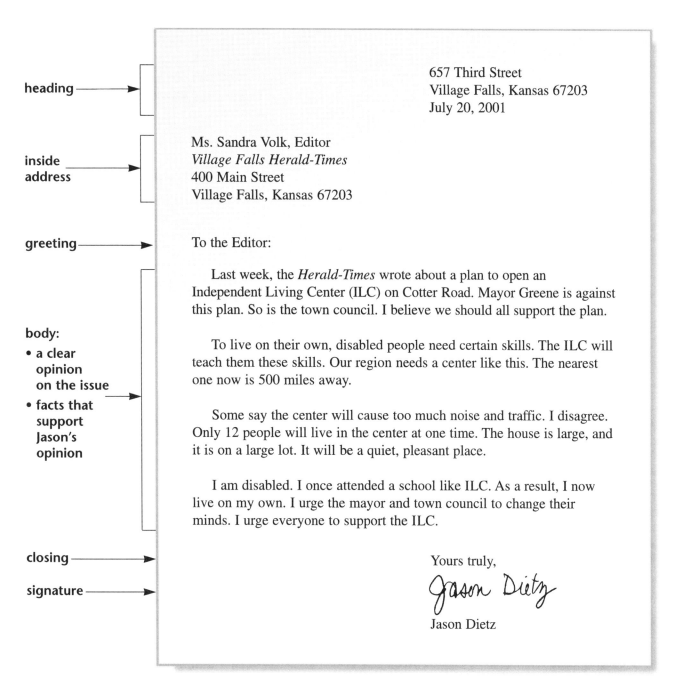

657 Third Street
Village Falls, Kansas 67203
July 20, 2001

Ms. Sandra Volk, Editor
Village Falls Herald-Times
400 Main Street
Village Falls, Kansas 67203

To the Editor:

Last week, the *Herald-Times* wrote about a plan to open an Independent Living Center (ILC) on Cotter Road. Mayor Greene is against this plan. So is the town council. I believe we should all support the plan.

To live on their own, disabled people need certain skills. The ILC will teach them these skills. Our region needs a center like this. The nearest one now is 500 miles away.

Some say the center will cause too much noise and traffic. I disagree. Only 12 people will live in the center at one time. The house is large, and it is on a large lot. It will be a quiet, pleasant place.

I am disabled. I once attended a school like ILC. As a result, I now live on my own. I urge the mayor and town council to change their minds. I urge everyone to support the ILC.

Yours truly,

Jason Dietz

Jason Dietz

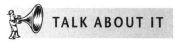

TALK ABOUT IT   What opinion does Jason state in his letter? What facts does he give to support his opinion?

TRY IT

Village Falls needs two new buses. The town has to decide whether to buy buses with special wheelchair lifts. The lifts are expensive—$15,000 each. In a news story, the mayor says he isn't sure if the lifts are needed. He want to know exactly how many people in town will use the lifts.

Jason writes to the editor. He says the lifts are needed. He points out that about 300 people in the area use wheelchairs. Many would ride buses if the buses had lifts.

Write Jason's letter to the editor. Use today's date. Jason's address is 657 Third Street, Village Falls, Kansas 67203. The editor's name is Sandra Volk. The newspaper, the *Village Falls Herald-Times,* is at 400 Main Street, Village Falls, Kansas 67203.

heading →

657 Third Street

_____

_____

inside address →

Ms. Sandra Volk, Editor

_____

_____

_____

greeting →

To the Editor:

body:
• a clear opinion on the issue
• facts that support Jason's opinion

Last week the *Herald-Times* wrote about the issues of buying new

buses with wheelchair lifts. _____

_____

_____

_____

_____

closing →

signature →

_____

Jason Dietz

Jason Dietz

Use the Checklist to see if your letter to the editor is clear and complete.

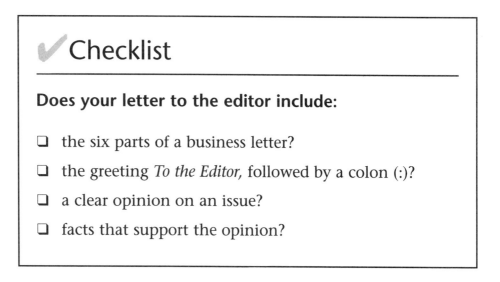

✔ Checklist

Does your letter to the editor include:

❑   the six parts of a business letter?

❑   the greeting *To the Editor,* followed by a colon (:)?

❑   a clear opinion on an issue?

❑   facts that support the opinion?

Is your letter to the editor clear and complete? Is there anything you would like to add or change? If so, go back and make the changes.

 USE IT

Think about the local issues you talked about at the beginning of the lesson. Choose one issue that you feel strongly about. How will you share your ideas? Write a letter to the editor of your local newspaper.

Use the space below to make some notes before you write your letter. Use the Checklist to help you. Be sure to state your opinion. Give facts to support your opinion.

Write a draft of your letter on a separate sheet of paper. Then prepare your final draft. Type it if you can. Save your letter to the editor in your portfolio.

Chapter 1

Apply It in the Real World

Speaking Out

Jason uses a wheelchair, but he has an active life. He works and plays sports. He has many friends. He takes part in community events. Here are some things Jason wants to do:

1. Last year, Jason got a new wheelchair. Now the motor loses power for no reason. Sometimes, it will not start. Jason has already written once to WheelTech Systems, the maker of the wheelchair. He explained the problem. He pointed out that the chair has a two-year guarantee. Jason wants the company to replace the chair. So far, however, the company has not answered his letter. WheelTech's address is 9104 Red Grove Road, Iowa City, Iowa 52240.

2. This summer Jason will visit a national park. He knows there is a booklet called the *National Park Guide for the Handicapped*. He thinks he can get it from the U.S. Government Printing Office. The address is Washington, D.C. 20402. He wants to ask about the booklet.

3. Many people in Village Falls are in favor of the Independent Living Center. That is a group home where disabled people will learn life skills. The town council finally approves the center. Jason wants to thank the people of Village Falls for supporting the center.

Decide and Write

A. Work with a group of classmates. Talk about each thing Jason wants to do. Remember what you learned about each type of business letter in Chapter 1. Then decide which type Jason should write for each situation.

B. Have each group member write one of the letters you need. Use the information above. Make up any other details you need. Remember that Jason's address is 657 Third Street, Village Falls, Kansas 67203. When you finish, save your work in your portfolio.

Completing Official Forms

Moving In, Moving On

Maddie and Tai want to rent an apartment. They are both 21 years old and live at home. They have jobs though. Together, they can afford an apartment. After weeks of looking, the two friends find a place. The apartment is in the town where they live now.

Maddie and Tai have to fill out many forms. To get the apartment, they fill out forms. They fill out forms at the post office. The two young women also register to vote. There are forms for that too.

The bus does not stop near their new apartment. So Maddie and Tai want to get a car. First, they each need a driver's license. That means filling out more forms.

Getting an apartment and a car are important to Maddie and Tai. Now they really feel part of their community!

Think About It

Think about these questions and discuss them with a partner. Then share your ideas with the class.

• What forms have you filled out lately?

• Why is it important to fill out a form neatly and completely?

• Why is it important that the facts on a form be correct?

Lesson 1 Rental Application Forms

Learning Objective

To rent an apartment or a house by filling out a rental application form

Words to Know

rental application form a form you fill out to rent an apartment or house

references people who can give information about you and your abilities

landlord the owner of an apartment or house for rent

 LEARN IT

Some day you will be on your own. You may want to get your own apartment. To do that, you may need to fill out a **rental application form**.

A rental application form asks many questions. You must give your name and address. You must tell where you work. The application may ask for **references**. References are people who know you well. They can tell someone if you are honest and if you will pay your bills. The **landlord**, the building's owner, might call your references to find out more about you.

When filling out any form, print neatly. Use a pen. Make sure you answer all the questions. Make sure the information you list is correct.

A rental application form should include:

- your name and address
- facts about your job
- the names of references

Why do landlords want to know about a renter's job? Why do they ask for references?

Maddie and Tai have found an apartment. They plan to share it. The landlord asks each of them to fill out a rental application form. Maddie has filled out the form below.

RENTAL APPLICATION FORM

name and address →

Name _____Swanson____Maddie_____P._____
                (last)   (first)   (middle initial)

Address _____2021 S. Overton Ave., Apt. 1B_____

_____Highland City, CA 97865_____

How long at present address? _____4 years_____

facts about Maddie's job →

Employer _____Sunset Home Industries_____

Employer
Address _____2250 Fuller Blvd._____

_____Highland City, CA 97865_____

How long at present job? __2 years__ Income __$325/week__

references →

Name of Reference _____Dan Izzo_____ Phone ___555-1129___

Name of Reference __Juanita Pierce__ Phone ___555-7721___

Do you plan to share this apartment with anyone? Yes _✓_ No ____

If yes, give the person's name. _____Tai L. Suzuki_____

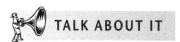 **TALK ABOUT IT**

What information did Maddie write about her job? How many people did she list as references?

TRY IT

Maddie will share the apartment with Tai L. Suzuki. Tai also has to fill out a rental application form. Tai's address is 1153 Wayland Street, Apartment 3, Highland City, California 97865. She has lived there four years.

Tai has worked for 20 months at the New Day Health Center. The address is 2002 Canyon Street in Highland City. She earns $350 a week as an aerobics teacher.

For references, Tai lists her boss, Ted Sung. His phone number is 555-1876. She also lists her high school English teacher, Emma Rosales. Her phone is 555-2898.

Fill in Tai's rental application. Remember to print with a pen.

RENTAL APPLICATION FORM

name
and
address

Name _____ _Suzuki_ _____
            (last)   (first)   (middle initial)

Address _____

_____

How long at present address? _____4 years_____

facts
about
Tai's
job

Employer _____New Day Health Center_____

Employer
Address _____

_____

How long at present job? _____ Income _____

references

Name of Reference ____Ted Sung____ Phone _____

Name of Reference _____ Phone _____

Do you plan to share this apartment with anyone? Yes ____ No ____

If yes, give the person's name. _____

Use the Checklist to make sure the rental application form is filled out correctly.

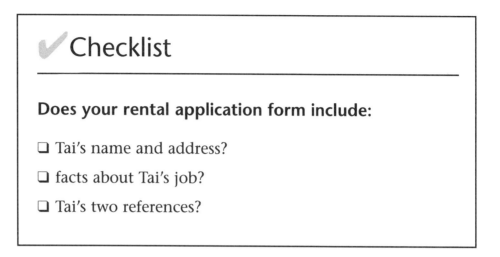

✔ Checklist

Does your rental application form include:

❑ Tai's name and address?

❑ facts about Tai's job?

❑ Tai's two references?

Did you leave any lines on the form blank? If so, go back and fill them in now.

 USE IT

Pretend you are renting an apartment. How will you do that? Fill out a rental application form.

Use the space below to make notes for your own form. Use real information about yourself when possible. Make up any other facts you need. Use the Checklist to help you.

Now fill in the Rental Application Form, which is Form 3A in *Forms in the Real World*. Save your completed form in your portfolio.

Lesson 2 | Change of Address Forms

Learning Objective

To change your mailing address by completing a post office form

Words to Know

change of address form a form that tells the post office
that you are moving

individual one person

temporary for a short time

 LEARN IT

The post office needs to know when you move. That way, it can forward, or send, mail to your new address. The post office will give you a **change of address form**.

First, you must print your name. On many forms, you must print your last name first. The form asks where you live now and where you plan to move to. It asks if just one **individual** is moving or if a whole family is moving. It asks when you will move to your new address. This date is called the *Start Date*. The form also asks if your new move is **temporary**, or if you plan to stay a long time.

A change of address form should include:

- the date you will move, or Start Date
- whether the form is for an individual or for a whole family
- whether the move is temporary or for a long time
- your last name, first name, and middle initial (if you have one)
- your old address and your new address
- your signature and the date

What might happen if you do not fill out a change of address form when you move? Why is it important to print everything carefully on the form?

LOOK AT IT

Maddie and Tai get the apartment they want. They cannot wait to move in. Maddie goes to the post office. She fills in a change of address form. She is filling in the form just for herself, not for her whole family. She plans to stay in her new apartment for a long time. When she moves, her mail will come to her new apartment.

how many people and date they will move

for short time or long time

name

old address

new address

signature and date

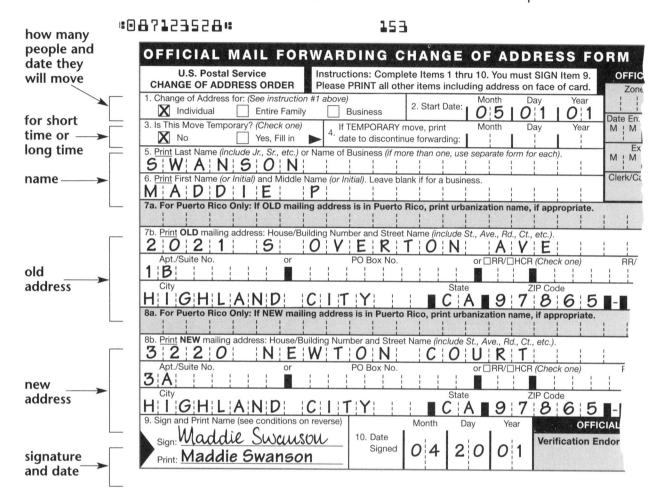

:087123528:   153

OFFICIAL MAIL FORWARDING CHANGE OF ADDRESS FORM

U.S. Postal Service
CHANGE OF ADDRESS ORDER

Instructions: Complete Items 1 thru 10. You must SIGN Item 9. Please PRINT all other items including address on face of card.

OFFIC
Zone

1. Change of Address for: (See instruction #1 above)
[X] Individual   [ ] Entire Family   [ ] Business

2. Start Date: Month 05 | Day 01 | Year 01

Date En.
M | M

3. Is This Move Temporary? (Check one)
[X] No   [ ] Yes, Fill in ▶

4. If TEMPORARY move, print date to discontinue forwarding: Month | Day | Year

Ex
M | M

5. Print Last Name (include Jr., Sr., etc.) or Name of Business (if more than one, use separate form for each).
S W A N S O N

Clerk/Ca

6. Print First Name (or Initial) and Middle Name (or Initial). Leave blank if for a business.
M A D D I E   P

7a. For Puerto Rico Only: If OLD mailing address is in Puerto Rico, print urbanization name, if appropriate.

7b. Print **OLD** mailing address: House/Building Number and Street Name (include St., Ave., Rd., Ct., etc.).
2 0 2 1   S   O V E R T O N   A V E

Apt./Suite No. 1 B   or   PO Box No.   or [ ]RR/[ ]HCR (Check one)   RR/

City H I G H L A N D   C I T Y   State C A   ZIP Code 9 7 8 6 5 -

8a. For Puerto Rico Only: If NEW mailing address is in Puerto Rico, print urbanization name, if appropriate.

8b. Print **NEW** mailing address: House/Building Number and Street Name (include St., Ave., Rd., Ct., etc.).
3 2 2 0   N E W T O N   C O U R T

Apt./Suite No. 3 A   or   PO Box No.   or [ ]RR/[ ]HCR (Check one)

City H I G H L A N D   C I T Y   State C A   ZIP Code 9 7 8 6 5 -

9. Sign and Print Name (see conditions on reverse)
Sign: *Maddie Swanson*
Print: **Maddie Swanson**

10. Date Signed: Month 04 | Day 20 | Year 01

OFFICIAL
Verification Endor

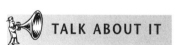

TALK ABOUT IT

How does Maddie know which numbers to write on line 2? How does she know which box to check on line 3?

TRY IT

Tai L. Suzuki fills out a change of address form on April 20, 2001. Her old address is 1153 Wayland Street, Apartment 3, Highland City, California 97865. Her new address is the same as Maddie's. However, Tai will not move into the new apartment until May 15. Like Maddie, she is filling in the form just for herself. She plans to stay in the new apartment for a long time.

Fill in the change of address form below for Tai. Print all the information in ink. Remember to fill in the Start Date. Finish by writing the date you signed the form.

how many
people and
date they
will move

for short
time or
long time

name

old
address

new
address

signature
and date

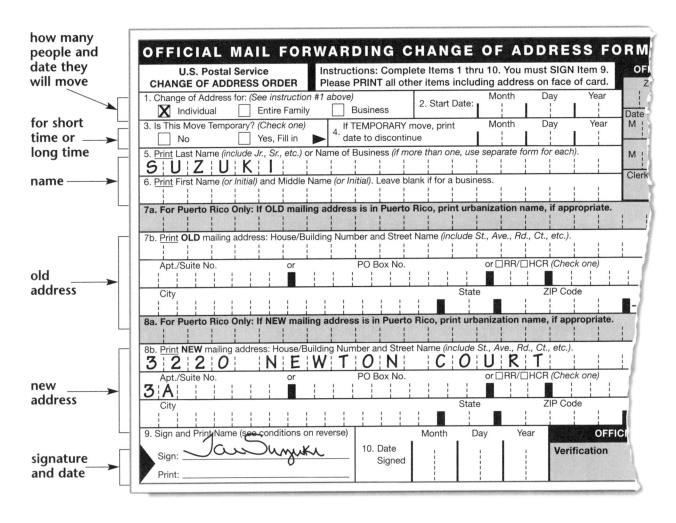

Use the Checklist to make sure you filled out the form correctly.

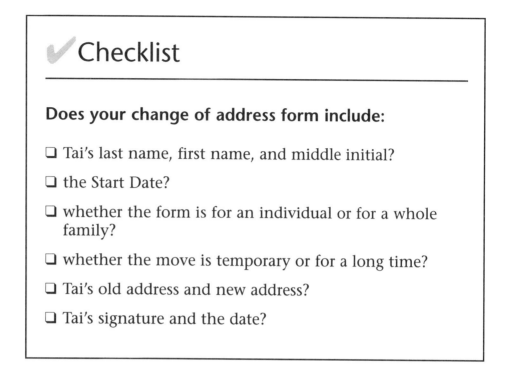

✔ Checklist

Does your change of address form include:

❑ Tai's last name, first name, and middle initial?

❑ the Start Date?

❑ whether the form is for an individual or for a whole family?

❑ whether the move is temporary or for a long time?

❑ Tai's old address and new address?

❑ Tai's signature and the date?

Did you print all the information the post office will need to forward Tai's mail? If not, go back and fill in any blanks you missed.

 USE IT

Pretend you are moving. How will you get mail at your new address? Fill in a change of address form.

Use the space below to make notes for your form. Make up a new address for yourself. Also make up a Start Date. Pretend that the form is just for you, not for your whole family. You plan to stay in your new apartment for a long time. You might note the items listed on the Checklist.

Now fill in the Change of Address Form, which is Form 4A in your *Forms in the Real World*. Save your completed form in your portfolio.

Lesson 3 Voter Registration Forms

Learning Objective

To sign up to vote by completing a voter registration form

Words to Know

register to sign up for something

voter registration form a form you must fill out to vote

 LEARN IT

Voting is part of being a good citizen. When you vote, your opinions count. You have a say in your community, state, and country.

You must **register** to vote. To register, fill out a **voter registration form**. You can get the form at post offices. The form asks for your name, address, and date of birth. It asks if you are a citizen of the United States. If you are *not* a U.S. citizen, do not fill out the form. You must tell if you have voted before or if you are registering for the first time. When you sign the form, you swear that the information is true. Lying on this form is a serious crime.

You can register to vote when you are 18 years old. If you move or change your name, you will have to register again. The form may ask if you would like to join a political party such as the Republicans or the Democrats. If you like, you may choose a party on the form.

A voter registration form should include:

- your name, address, and date of birth
- a mark showing if you are a citizen of the United States
- a mark showing if you have voted before
- a choice of political party, if you wish
- your signature and the date

How can voting help you take part in your community?

LOOK AT IT

On May 1, Maddie moves into her new apartment. A few days later, she registers to vote. At the post office, she gets a voter registration form. She fills out all the lines on the form. Then she mails it to the Board of Elections, an agency that runs elections.

A few weeks later, the Board of Elections sends Maddie a card. She is registered. The card tells her where to vote. Next Election Day, in November, Maddie will be able to vote.

Here is the voter registration form Maddie fills out:

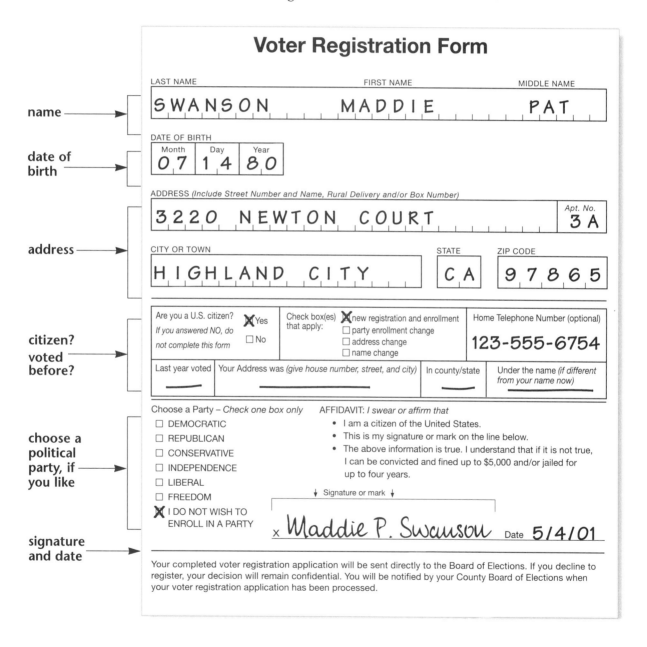

TALK ABOUT IT

Why did Maddie draw lines through four boxes on the form? What promises did she make by signing the form?

 **TRY IT**

Tai Suzuki moves into the new apartment with Maddie. Tai decides to register too. Tai's middle name is Lisa. Her address is the same as Maddie's. Tai was born on August 8, 1980. Tai is a U.S. citizen. This is the first time she has registered to vote. Her phone number is 123-555-6754. Tai decides to join the Democratic Party.

Fill out the voter registration form for Tai. Use the information above.

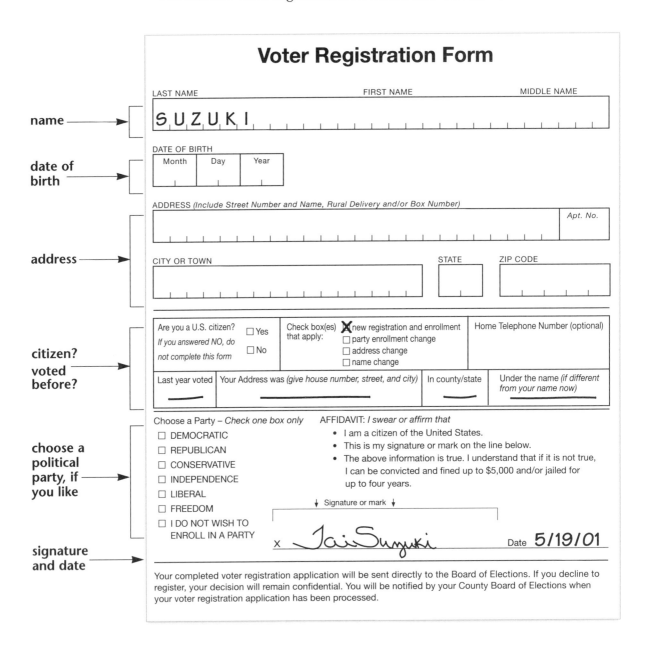

Voter Registration Form

name

LAST NAME | FIRST NAME | MIDDLE NAME
S U Z U K I

date of birth

DATE OF BIRTH
Month | Day | Year

address

ADDRESS (Include Street Number and Name, Rural Delivery and/or Box Number) | Apt. No.

CITY OR TOWN | STATE | ZIP CODE

citizen? voted before?

Are you a U.S. citizen? ☐ Yes ☐ No
If you answered NO, do not complete this form

Check box(es) that apply: ☒ new registration and enrollment ☐ party enrollment change ☐ address change ☐ name change

Home Telephone Number (optional)

Last year voted | Your Address was (give house number, street, and city) | In county/state | Under the name (if different from your name now)

choose a political party, if you like

Choose a Party – Check one box only
☐ DEMOCRATIC
☐ REPUBLICAN
☐ CONSERVATIVE
☐ INDEPENDENCE
☐ LIBERAL
☐ FREEDOM
☐ I DO NOT WISH TO ENROLL IN A PARTY

AFFIDAVIT: I swear or affirm that
• I am a citizen of the United States.
• This is my signature or mark on the line below.
• The above information is true. I understand that if it is not true, I can be convicted and fined up to $5,000 and/or jailed for up to four years.

↓ Signature or mark ↓

signature and date

x _Tai Suzuki_   Date **5/19/01**

Your completed voter registration application will be sent directly to the Board of Elections. If you decline to register, your decision will remain confidential. You will be notified by your County Board of Elections when your voter registration application has been processed.

Use the Checklist to see if you filled out the voter registration form completely.

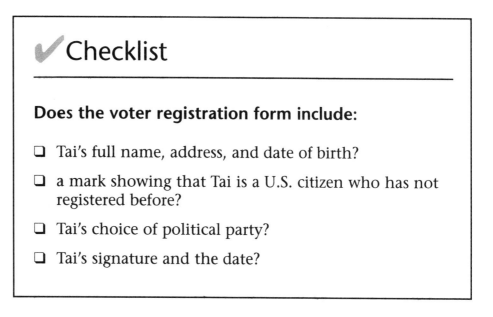

✔ **Checklist**

Does the voter registration form include:

❑ Tai's full name, address, and date of birth?

❑ a mark showing that Tai is a U.S. citizen who has not registered before?

❑ Tai's choice of political party?

❑ Tai's signature and the date?

Is there anything you have left out of the form? If so, go back and fill it in.

USE IT

Pretend that you are registering to vote. How will you do that? Fill out a voter registration form.

Use the space below to make notes for your form. Even if you are not 18 years old yet, it will be good practice. You should know all the facts that the form asks. You might note the items listed on the Checklist.

Now fill in the Voter Registration Form, which is Form 5A in *Forms in the Real World*. Save your completed form in your portfolio.

Lesson 4 Driver's License Applications

Learning Objective
To get your driver's license by completing an application

Words to Know
learner's permit a special license for people who are learning to drive

driver's license a card that lets you drive a car legally

 LEARN IT

Each state has its own rules for drivers. However, in all states, you need a **learner's permit** to learn how to drive. When you know how to drive, you can apply for a **driver's license**. A driver's license lets you drive a car legally. A license also proves who you are. It is a form of identification, or I.D. To get a license, you must take a road test. During the road test, someone will sit beside you to judge how well you drive.

The application for a driver's license asks for information about you. You must print your name, address, and date of birth. You must also print your sex, height, eye color, and Social Security number. It may ask about your health too. The form may ask you about your driving record as well.

If you do not understand these questions, ask the clerk at the Office of Motor Vehicles. Be sure to answer all questions truthfully and sign your name at the bottom of the form. Print neatly with a pen.

An application for a driver's license should include:

- your name, address, and date of birth
- your sex, height, eye color, and Social Security number
- facts about your health and driving record
- your signature

Why do you think people must have a license to drive?

After getting her learner's permit, Maddie learns to drive. Now she wants to apply for a driver's license. She wants to take a road test too. Maddie goes to the Office of Motor Vehicles and fills out the application.

Here is the driver's license application that Maddie fills out.

APPLICATION FOR DRIVER LICENSE *"OR"* NON-DRIVER ID CARD

name →

LAST NAME	FIRST NAME	MIDDLE NAME
S W A N S O N	M A D D I E	P A T

facts about Maddie →

DATE OF BIRTH			SEX	HEIGHT		EYE COLOR	SOCIAL SECURITY NUMBER (SSN)
Month 0 7	Day 1 4	Year 8 0	M ☐ F ☒	Ft. 5	Inches 0 9	B L	0 3 2 0 1 7 5 4 3

address →

ADDRESS WHERE YOU LIVE — *DO NOT GIVE P.O. BOX (Include Street Number and Name, Rural Delivery, and/or Box Number)*

3 2 2 0 N E W T O N C O U R T	Apt. No. 3 A

CITY OR TOWN	STATE	ZIP CODE
H I G H L A N D C I T Y	C A	9 7 8 6 5

facts about Maddie's health →

1. Do you need to wear corrective lenses while operating a motor vehicle? ☒ Yes ☐ No
   Removal of a corrective lens restriction from your license can only be done in a Motor Vehicles office.
2. Have you had, or are you being treated for, any of the following, or has a previous disability worsened? ☒ Yes ☐ No
   If "Yes," check all that apply.
   ☐ 1. Convulsive disorder, epilepsy, fainting or dizzy spells, or any condition which causes unconsciousness
   ☐ 2. Heart ailment
   ☒ 3. Hearing impairment
   ☐ 4. Lost use of leg, arm, foot, hand, or eye
   ☐ 5. Other (explain) _____
   If you checked box 1 or 2, obtain the appropriate medical form from a Motor Vehicles office. The form must be completed by you and your physician.

facts about Maddie's driving record →

3. Have you had a driver license, permit, or privilege to operate a motor vehicle suspended, revoked or cancelled, or an application for a license denied in this state or elsewhere? ☐ Yes ☒ No
   If "Yes," has your license, permit or privilege been restored or your application approved? ☐ Yes ☐ No
4. Have you been found guilty of a traffic infraction (except parking violations) or vehicle-related crime or offense, or forfeited bail in any such case in any court either in this state or elsewhere within the past 5 years? ☐ Yes ☒ No
   If "Yes," give details below. If more space is needed, attach an additional sheet.

Date *(Mo/Day/Yr)*	Crime, or Offense	Court & Location
/ /		
/ /		

CERTIFICATION I, the undersigned, state that the information I have given on this application is true to the best of my knowledge.

signature →

SIGN HERE ▶ *Maddie P. Swanson*
(Sign name in full. A married woman must use her own first name.)

IMPORTANT Making a false statement in any license or non-driver ID card application or in any proof or statement in connection with it is a misdemeanor, and may result in the revocation or suspension of your license or non-driver ID card.

 **TALK ABOUT IT**

What information about herself did Maddie print in the boxes? Why did Maddie answer *No* in the boxes for questions 3 and 4?

 **TRY IT**

Maddie passes her road test and gets her driver's license. Now Maddie's friend Tai wants to get a driver's license too. Tai is ready for a road test. First, she fills out an application for a driver's license.

Tai's full name is Tai Lisa Suzuki. Her address is the same as Maddie's. Tai was born on August 8, 1980. She has brown eyes. Her height is 5 feet 6 inches. Her Social Security number is 038-76-0989. Tai does not wear glasses. She is not being treated for any of the disabilities on the form either. Tai also answers *No* to questions 3 and 4.

Fill out the application for Tai. Use the information above.

APPLICATION FOR DRIVER LICENSE *"OR"* NON-DRIVER ID CARD

name →

LAST NAME | **FIRST NAME** | **MIDDLE NAME**

S U Z U K I

facts about Tai →

DATE OF BIRTH — Month | Day | Year
SEX M ☐ F ☒
HEIGHT Ft. | Inches
EYE COLOR
SOCIAL SECURITY NUMBER (SSN)

address →

ADDRESS WHERE YOU LIVE — *DO NOT GIVE P.O. BOX (Include Street Number and Name, Rural Delivery, and/or Box Number)*

3 2 2 0   N E W T O N   C O U R T

Apt. # 3A

CITY OR TOWN | **STATE** | **ZIP CODE**

facts about Tai's health →

1. Do you need to wear corrective lenses while operating a motor vehicle? ☐Yes ☐No
Removal of a corrective lens restriction from your license can only be done in a Motor Vehicles office.
2. Have you had, or are you being treated for, any of the following, or has a previous disability worsened? ☐Yes ☐No
If "Yes," check all that apply.
   ☐ 1. Convulsive disorder, epilepsy, fainting or dizzy spells, or any condition which causes unconsciousness
   ☐ 2. Heart ailment
   ☐ 3. Hearing impairment
   ☐ 4. Lost use of leg, arm, foot, hand, or eye
   ☐ 5. Other (explain) _____
   If you checked box 1 or 2, obtain the appropriate medical form from a Motor Vehicles office. The form must be completed by you and your physician.

facts about Tai's driving record →

3. Have you had a driver license, permit, or privilege to operate a motor vehicle suspended, revoked or cancelled, or an application for a license denied in this state or elsewhere? ☐Yes ☐No
If "Yes," has your license, permit or privilege been restored or your application approved? ☐Yes ☐No
4. Have you been found guilty of a traffic infraction (except parking violations) or vehicle-related crime or offense, or forfeited bail in any such case in any court either in this state or elsewhere within the past 5 years? ☐Yes ☐No
If "Yes," give details below. If more space is needed, attach an additional sheet.

Date *(Mo/Day/Yr)*	Crime, or Offense	Court & Location
/ /		
/ /		

CERTIFICATION I, the undersigned, state that the information I have given on this application is true to the best of my knowledge.

signature →

SIGN HERE ▶ *Tai Suzuki*
(Sign name in full. A married woman must use her own first name.)

Use the Checklist to see if you filled out the application completely.

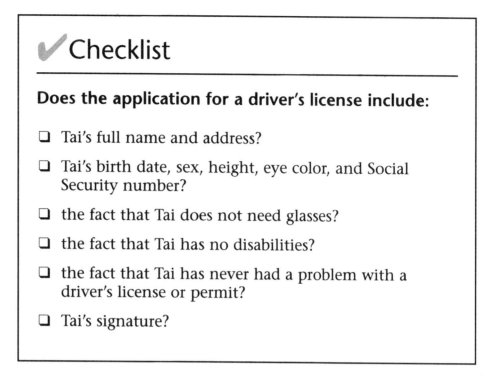

✔ Checklist

Does the application for a driver's license include:

❑ Tai's full name and address?

❑ Tai's birth date, sex, height, eye color, and Social Security number?

❑ the fact that Tai does not need glasses?

❑ the fact that Tai has no disabilities?

❑ the fact that Tai has never had a problem with a driver's license or permit?

❑ Tai's signature?

Is there anything you have left out of the form? If so, go back and fill it in.

 USE IT   Pretend that you are applying for a driver's license. How will you do that? Fill out a driver's license application.

Use the space below to make notes for your application. Use real information about yourself if you can. You might note the items listed on the Checklist.

Now fill in the Driver's License Application, which is Form 6A in *Forms in the Real World*. Save your completed application in your portfolio.

Chapter 2

Apply It in the Real World

A Place of Their Own

A small apartment on Maddie's and Tai's floor is empty. Tai tells her friend Kris to look at it. Kris works with Maddie at Sunset Home Industries. She likes the apartment. Kris has never moved to her own place before. She is not sure what she needs to do.

Here are some of the things Kris needs to do:

1. Kris wants her mail sent to her new address. Her new address is 3220 Newton Court, Apartment 9B, Highland City, California 97865. Her old address is 150 Oak Street, Highland City, CA 97865. She wants her mail sent there beginning on June 15, when she will move in. She is not sure what to do about this though.

2. Kris goes to see the landlord of the building. She finds out that she has to fill out a form. She is not sure what the form is called. She does not know what facts she needs for the form either.

3. Kris does not want to miss her chance to vote in November. What does she have to do to vote at her new address?

4. Kris has already learned to drive, but she does not have a license yet. What form must she fill out before she can drive on her own?

Decide and Write

A. In a small group, discuss each thing Kris wants to do. Decide which types of forms from Chapter 2 will help Kris reach her goals. Remember what you learned about each form. What types of information will Kris need for the forms?

B. Each group member can choose one form to fill out for Kris. Use the forms in *Forms in the Real World*. You can find information about Kris in the description above and in the chapter. Make up any other details you need. Save your work in your portfolio.

Unit Three

WRAP-UP

In Unit Three, you practiced writing different types of business letters. In years to come, you will write letters like these as you take part in your community. You also worked on filling out forms. When you are ready to live on your own, you will need to fill out forms like these.

WRITING for the COMMUNITY

Writing Letters

- Letters of Inquiry
- Letters of Complaint
- Letters to the Editor

Completing Official Forms

- Rental Application Forms
- Change of Address Forms
- Voter Registration Forms
- Driver's License Applications

Read the lists of writing types on the chart. Choose two types of writing. Then, on the lines below, describe a time in your own life when you may need to use each type of writing.

1. _____

_____

2. _____

_____

What Did You Learn?

On page 72, you listed some ways in which you use writing in your community. Look again at this list. Can you think of more types of writing to add to the list? What forms might you add?

Unit Four

SHOPPING and MANAGING MONEY

Shopping is easy for most of us. Managing money takes more effort. Both activities go together though. They also play a major part in our lives. Having a bank account is part of managing money. In this unit, you will fill out forms to open and use bank accounts. Forms also help you shop. Whether you are applying for a credit card, buying by mail, or placing a classified ad in a newspaper, you will need to fill out forms.

In Unit Four, you will learn how to shop and manage your money.

Chapter 1   **Banking**

Chapter 2   **Buying and Selling**

What Do You Know?

Work with a group of classmates. Discuss what you know about bank accounts and shopping. List some types of writing that might help you open and use a bank account. Also list different ways in which people buy things. Save your lists to use later.

Banking

Making Money

Ali Tamiz buys a box of old books at a yard sale. The books are from the 1800s. Ali does not know much about old books. He just thinks these books look unusual. He decides to pay $20 for the box.

Ali shows the books to a dealer in town. The dealer is excited. He says that two of the books are very rare. They are in fine condition too. The dealer wants to buy the books. He offers Ali $1,200 for the two books. Ali decides to sell them.

Ali has never had so much money. He decides to open his first bank account. At the bank, Ali fills out an application. Soon he has his own checking account. Ali puts some money into the account. The bank gives him his own checks. Now Ali can write checks when he wants to buy things. He can use a cash machine too. Having a checking account helps Ali keep track of his money.

Ali is buying more things at yard sales now. He hopes to find another treasure.

Think About It

Think about these questions and discuss them with a partner. Then share your ideas with the class.

• How can a bank account help you manage your money?

• Why is it important to know how much money you have in a checking account?

• When might it be useful to buy something with a check?

Lesson 1 Bank Account Applications

Learning Objective

To open a bank account by filling out an application

Words to Know

checking account money in a bank that can be taken out by using a check

savings account money in a bank that gains interest

 LEARN IT

Many people have **checking accounts.** Using checks to pay bills is easy and safe. A checking account also helps you keep track of your money.

A **savings account** is another type of bank account. You cannot write checks with a savings account. A bank pays you interest for keeping your money in a savings account. That means the bank adds a little bit of its own money to your account each month.

To apply for a checking or savings account, you must fill out a bank account application. The bank will ask you for your full name, address, and date of birth. By law, the bank needs your Social Security number too. Print clearly in ink.

The bank will ask for your signature, or your signed name. You must sign your name the same way every time you write a check. The bank files this authorized, or approved, signature. That way, the bank will know if someone else tries to use your checks.

An application for a bank account should include:

- what kind of account you want to open
- your name, address, phone number, birth date, and Social Security number
- how much money you plan to put in the account
- your authorized signature

Why might you want to use a checking account? Why might you want to use a savings account?

 **LOOK AT IT**

Ali makes $1,200 by selling some old books. He decides to open a checking account at Union Bank. On November 2, Ali opens the account. He decides to put $900 in the checking account. To open his checking account, Ali fills out the bank account application below.

◆ Union Bank

BANK ACCOUNT APPLICATION

kind of account ——▶ Type of Account: ✓ Checking ____ Savings

how much money Ali plans to put into the account ——▶ Date Opened: November 2, 2001

Initial Deposit: $900

authorized signature ——▶ Authorized Signature: *Ali Tamiz*

name ——▶ Name: Ali Tamiz

address ——▶ Address: 211 Schoolhouse Road

Payton, NJ 08550

phone number ——▶ Home Phone: 201-555-6773

birth date ——▶ Date of Birth: 6/10/84

Social Security number ——▶ Social Security Number: 101-01-1796

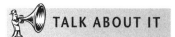 **TALK ABOUT IT**

What information must you write on a bank account application? Why did Ali print his name on the *Name* line? Why did he write it differently on the *Authorized Signature* line?

 **TRY IT**

Ali also opens a savings account at Union Bank. He opens it on the same day. He puts the rest of his money—$300—into this account. He has to fill out a second application for this account.

Fill out Ali's application for a savings account. Use the same information shown on page 109. Remember to print with a pen.

☘ **Union Bank**

BANK ACCOUNT APPLICATION

kind of account ➔   Type of Account: _____ Checking _____ Savings

how much money Ali plans to put into the account ➔   Date Opened: _____ November 2, 2001 _____

Initial Deposit: _____

authorized signature ➔   Authorized Signature: _*Ali Famiz*_ _____

name ➔   Name: _____

address ➔   Address: _____

_____

phone number ➔   Home Phone: _____

birth date ➔   Date of Birth: _____

Social Security number ➔   Social Security Number: _____

Use the Checklist to make sure you filled out the application correctly.

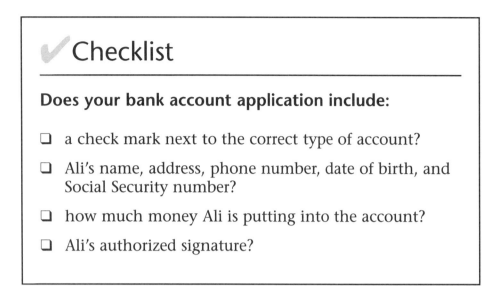

Did you leave any lines on the form blank? If so, go back and fill them in now.

 USE IT   Imagine you want to open a bank account. What do you need to do? Decide if you would like a checking account or a savings account. Then fill in a bank account application form.

Prepare a draft of your application in the space below.

Use the Checklist to make sure your application is complete. Now fill in the Bank Account Application, which is Form 7A in *Forms in the Real World*. Save your completed application in your portfolio.

Lesson 2 Bank Checks

Learning Objective

To pay bills by filling out a bank check

Words to Know

authorized signature signed name that the bank keeps on file

LEARN IT

When you put money into a checking account, you can write checks. Each check you write takes money out of your account.

Begin by writing the date in the upper-right corner of the check. Next, write the name of the person who will get the check next to *Pay to the Order of*. You must write the amount twice. First use numbers next to the dollar ($) sign. On the line below, write the amount in words. Next to the word *Memo* at the bottom of your check, note what the check is for. Then sign the check on the bottom-right corner. A check cannot be cashed without an **authorized signature**.

A check should include:

- the date and the name of who the check is for

- the amount of the check in both numbers and words

- the authorized signature of the person writing the check

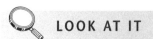

LOOK AT IT   After he opens his checking account, Ali writes this check.

 **TALK ABOUT IT**   Who will receive this check? How much is the check for?

 **TRY IT**   On November 28, 2001, Ali buys an old painting at a flea market. He pays $65 for the painting. Ali buys the painting from Milton Flowers. Ali makes out the check to Mr. Flowers.

Fill in the check for Ali.

who the check is for

amount in words

what the check is for

date

amount in numbers

authorized signature

Use the Checklist to make sure you filled out the check correctly.

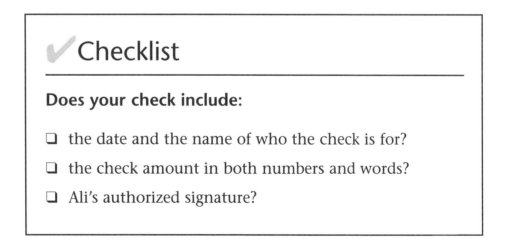

✔ Checklist

Does your check include:

❑ the date and the name of who the check is for?

❑ the check amount in both numbers and words?

❑ Ali's authorized signature?

 USE IT   Imagine you would like to buy something using a check. What will you buy? Will you buy it in a store or from a person? Fill in the Bank Check, which is Form 8A in *Forms in the Real World*. Use the Checklist to make sure your check is complete. Save your check in your portfolio.

Lesson 3 Deposits and Withdrawals

Learning Objective

To make bank deposits and withdrawals by filling out slips

Words to Know

deposit money you put into a bank account

deposit slip form you fill out to put money into a bank account

withdrawal money you take out of a bank account

 LEARN IT

Sometimes people add money to their checking account. This is called making a **deposit.** To make a deposit, fill out a **deposit slip.** Your bank will give you deposit slips with your name and account number printed on them.

On the deposit slip, write the date. If your deposit is cash, write the amount on the *Cash* line. If your deposit is a check or a few checks, write the amount of each check. Add up all the cash and checks. Write that amount on the *Net Deposit* line.

Sometimes people take money out of their savings account. This is called making a **withdrawal.** To make a withdrawal, fill out a withdrawal slip. Write the date and your account number. Also write the exact amount you want to withdraw, in both numbers and words. You will have to sign the withdrawal slip.

When you fill out these forms, use a pen and print clearly. Make sure you write all numbers clearly too.

A deposit or withdrawal slip should include:

- the date
- your name and your account number
- the amount of the deposit or withdrawal

When might you make a deposit into your checking account? Why might you make a withdrawal from your savings account?

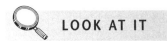 **LOOK AT IT**

Ali bought an old painting at a flea market for $65. Now an art dealer in town wants to buy it. She gives Ali a check for $250. Ali goes to the bank. He fills out a deposit slip for the check. Ali also has $30 in cash to put into his checking account. Here is the deposit slip Ali fills out.

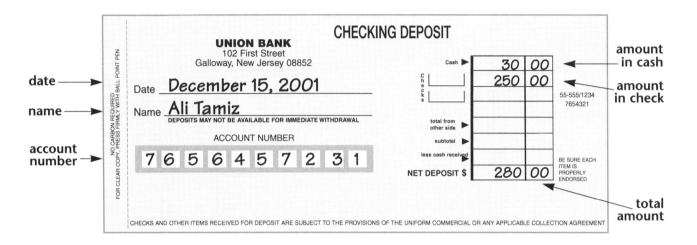

Late in December, Ali has a chance to buy a set of books. To pay for them, he needs to make a withdrawal from his savings account. Here is the withdrawal slip he fills out.

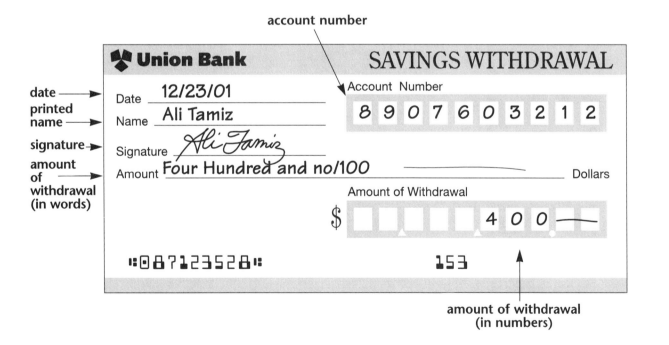

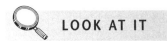 **TALK ABOUT IT**

What was the total deposit that Ali made into his checking account? How much money did Ali take out of his savings account?

TRY IT

Ali continues to buy things at yard sales and flea markets. He enjoys doing this. He makes money at it too. He usually pays with checks. When Ali sells things, people give him checks. Ali usually deposits his checks right into his checking account. On February 3, 2002, Ali deposits three checks into his account. One is for $130. The others are for $55 and $30. Fill in the deposit slip below for Ali. His account number is 7656457231.

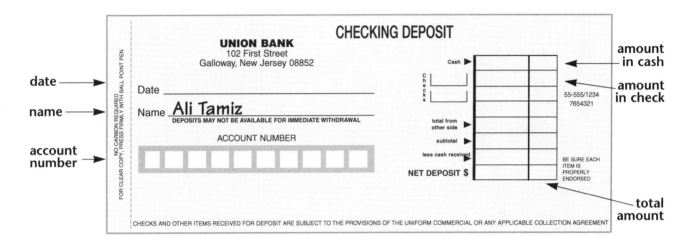

On March 13, 2002, Ali needs to make a withdrawal from his savings account. His savings account number is 8907603212. The amount of the withdrawal is $250. Fill in the withdrawal slip below.

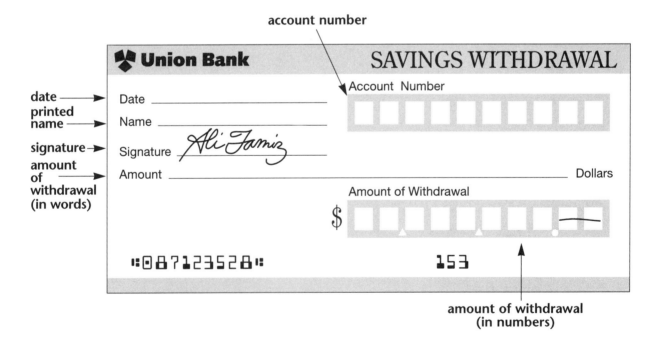

Use the Checklist below. Make sure you filled out the deposit slip and the withdrawal slip correctly.

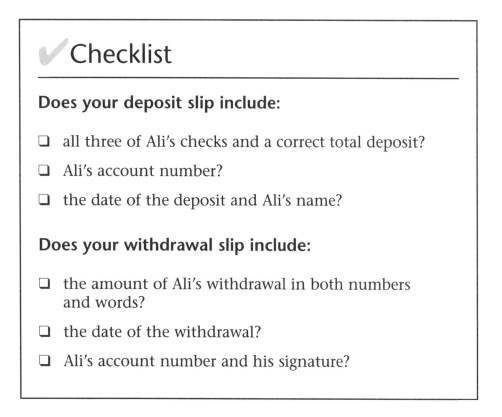

✔ Checklist

Does your deposit slip include:

❑ all three of Ali's checks and a correct total deposit?

❑ Ali's account number?

❑ the date of the deposit and Ali's name?

Does your withdrawal slip include:

❑ the amount of Ali's withdrawal in both numbers and words?

❑ the date of the withdrawal?

❑ Ali's account number and his signature?

Did you fill out the slips completely? If not, complete them now.

 USE IT

Pretend you are going with Ali to his next flea market. You want to sell some old chairs and maybe buy something for yourself.

You decide to withdraw some money from your savings account in case you see something you want to buy. Decide how much to withdraw and then fill in the Bank Withdrawal form, which is Form 10A in *Forms in the Real World*. Use the Checklist to make sure your slip is complete.

At the end of the day at the flea market, you finally sell your chairs. You get $85 in cash for them. Fill in the Bank Deposit, which is Form 9A in *Forms in the Real World*, to deposit the cash into your checking account. Use the Checklist to make sure your slip is complete.

Save both completed slips in your portfolio.

Lesson 4 Check Registers

Learning Objective

To keep track of your money by using a check register

Words to Know

check register a booklet to keep track of your balance

LEARN IT

A **check register** tells how much money is in your checking account. When you write a check, record it in your check register. The letters *ATM* stand for "Automated Teller Machine." A withdrawal from an ATM is like writing a check or making a withdrawal. Each time you make an ATM withdrawal, subtract the amount from your balance. Then write the new balance in your check register. When you make a deposit, add the amount to your balance. Then write the new balance.

A check register should include:

- the date and amount of each deposit, check, or ATM withdrawal

- the check number of each check you write

- the person or business each check is for

- the balance of your account

LOOK AT IT

Here is part of Ali's check register. He has written a check for $24 and made an ATM withdrawal of $40. He has deposited $75.

check number	date	who check is for	check amounts	deposit amounts	balance	

PLEASE BE SURE TO DEDUCT ANY CHECK CHARGES OR SERVICE CHARGES THAT MAY APPLY TO YOUR ACCOUNT

NUMBER	DATE	CHECKS ISSUED TO OR DESCRIPTION OF DEPOSIT	(–) AMOUNT OF CHECK		(+) AMOUNT OF DEPOSIT		BALANCE	
							1,320	00
107	11/29	Harley's Dept. Store	24	00			1,296	00
	11/30	ATM withdrawal	40	00			1,256	00
	11/30	Check from Book Sale			75	00	1,331	00

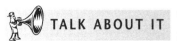 **TALK ABOUT IT** On what date did Ali write a check for $24? How did Ali get the money to make a $75 deposit?

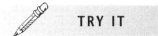 **TRY IT** Ali is having fun buying and selling. On December 1, he writes a check for $80 to Elton Pertwell. The number of the check is 122. He also makes an ATM withdrawal for $50 that day. Later that day he sells some books. He receives a check for $120, which he deposits.

Use these facts to fill in Ali's check register. His balance is $1,420.

check number	date	who check is for	check amounts	deposit amounts	balance

PLEASE BE SURE TO DEDUCT ANY CHECK CHARGES OR SERVICE CHARGES THAT MAY APPLY TO YOUR ACCOUNT

NUMBER	DATE	CHECKS ISSUED TO OR DESCRIPTION OF DEPOSIT	(−) AMOUNT OF CHECK	(+) AMOUNT OF DEPOSIT	BALANCE	
					1,420	00
122	12/1	Elton Pertwell				
	12/1	ATM—cash				
	12/1	Deposit—sale of books				

Reminder

Add each deposit to your balance. Subtract each withdrawal.

Use the Checklist to see if you filled out the check register correctly.

✔ **Checklist**

Does the check register include:

❑ the date and amount of each deposit, check, or ATM withdrawal Ali made?

❑ the check number of each check Ali wrote?

❑ the person or business each check was for?

❑ a new balance?

 USE IT Imagine you have a balance of $450 in your checking account. What checks would you like to write? Fill out the Check Register, which is Form 11A in *Forms in the Real World*. Write the date, check number, and amount of each check. Write the name of the person or business who will receive the check. Use the Checklist to make sure the check register is complete. Save your completed check register in your portfolio.

Apply It in the Real World

Managing Money

Ali's bank accounts make it easy for him to manage his money. His savings account is a safe place to keep money. His checking account makes it easy to pay bills and buy things. Here are some ways that Ali uses his two bank accounts this month:

1. Ali earns $250 selling books at a flea market. What should Ali do to put the money in his checking account?

2. Ali wants to buy a glass vase for $50 at a yard sale. The owner will not take a check though. Ali goes to the bank to get cash. He would like to take the money from his savings account. How should he do that?

3. At King Groceries, Ali buys $45 of food. He does not have that much cash in his wallet. How else can Ali pay for the food?

4. At the end of one day, Ali is not sure what the balance is in his checking account. He wrote two checks that day for $50 and $130. He also made a deposit of $100. His balance at the beginning of the day is $980. What should Ali do to figure out his new balance?

5. A new bank opens in Ali's town. This bank pays more interest on savings accounts than Ali's bank does. Ali decides to put his savings in the new bank. What will he have to do?

Decide and Write

A. In a small group, discuss what Ali must do in each situation. If he needs to fill out a form, decide which one he needs.

B. Have each member of your group fill out one of the forms Ali needs. Use the forms in *Forms in the Real World*. Find information about Ali in the description above and in the chapter. Make up any other details you need. Save your work in your portfolio.

Chapter 2

Buying and Selling

Going Camping

Terri and Jenelle have never gone camping. That is about to change though. The two friends have decided to go backpacking this summer.

The young women will be in the mountains alone for more than a week. They want the trip to go well, so they are planning it carefully.

Getting the right equipment is very important. They need a tent, sleeping bags, and hiking boots. To find the right equipment, Terri and Jenelle have to shop.

Both young women want to get credit cards. That way, they can charge some of the things they need. They also plan to buy some things from catalogs. Terri has a few catalogs that sell camping equipment. Jenelle plans to order some things on the Internet. When she gets her credit card, Internet shopping will be easy.

Jenelle also reads classified ads in the local newspaper. Many people try to sell used camping equipment there. By checking newspaper ads, she can find things she needs.

Think About It

Think about these questions and discuss them with a partner. Then share your ideas with the class.

- What do you have to think about when you shop with a credit card?

- Do you ever order things from catalogs? How is it different from buying something at a store?

- Why is a classified ad a good way to buy or sell used equipment?

Lesson 1 — Credit Card Applications

Learning Objective

To apply for a credit card by filling out an application

Words to Know

credit money borrowed from a bank or store to buy things

credit card a card you can use to buy things without paying for them right away

LEARN IT

Credit is money that you borrow from a bank or store to buy things. You pay the money back later. A **credit card** is an easy way to use credit. Banks and stores offer credit cards. With a credit card, you do not have to carry cash. You can also buy things by phone with a credit card.

To apply for a credit card, you fill out an application. The form asks for your name, address, and phone number. It also asks for your birth date and Social Security number.

You also have to give facts about your job and how much money you earn. The form asks about your checking or savings accounts too. You must also tell how much rent or mortgage you pay. The application may also ask personal information such as your mother's maiden name. After filling out the form, you must sign it. By signing, you promise to pay your bill each month.

Reminder

Banks and stores charge high interest on money you do not pay back right away. You need to be careful how you use credit cards.

An application for a credit card should include:

- your name, address, phone number, birth date, and Social Security number
- facts about your job and how much you earn
- facts about your bank accounts
- facts about your home and your rent
- personal information such as your mother's maiden name
- your signature

What are some ways that people use credit cards?

 **LOOK AT IT**

Terri needs to buy camping equipment. She decides to buy some of it on credit, so she fills out this application for a credit card. Notice what information she lists.

name →

Social Security number →

address →

Terri's job →

signature →

birth date

phone number

rent

how much Terri earns

Terri's bank accounts

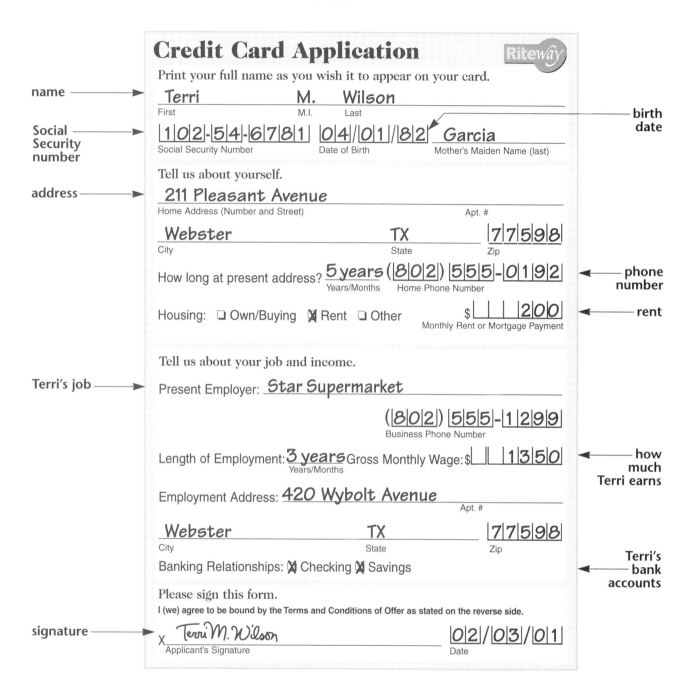

Credit Card Application

Riteway

Print your full name as you wish it to appear on your card.

Terri   M.   Wilson
First   M.I.   Last

|1|0|2|-|5|4|-|6|7|8|1| |0|4|/|0|1|/|8|2| Garcia
Social Security Number   Date of Birth   Mother's Maiden Name (last)

Tell us about yourself.

211 Pleasant Avenue
Home Address (Number and Street)   Apt. #

Webster   TX |7|7|5|9|8|
City   State   Zip

How long at present address? 5 years (|8|0|2|) |5|5|5|-|0|1|9|2|
                            Years/Months   Home Phone Number

Housing: ☐ Own/Buying ☒ Rent ☐ Other $| | |2|0|0|
                                            Monthly Rent or Mortgage Payment

Tell us about your job and income.

Present Employer: Star Supermarket

(|8|0|2|) |5|5|5|-|1|2|9|9|
Business Phone Number

Length of Employment: 3 years Gross Monthly Wage: $| | |1|3|5|0|
                      Years/Months

Employment Address: 420 Wybolt Avenue
                                        Apt. #

Webster   TX |7|7|5|9|8|
City   State   Zip

Banking Relationships: ☒ Checking ☒ Savings

Please sign this form.
I (we) agree to be bound by the Terms and Conditions of Offer as stated on the reverse side.

X _Terri M. Wilson_ _____ |0|2|/|0|3|/|0|1|
Applicant's Signature   Date

TALK ABOUT IT

What information does Terri write on the credit card application form? By signing her name, what promise is Terri making?

TRY IT

Jenelle also applies for a credit card. Her last name is Stone. Her address is 678 Hereford Drive, Webster, Texas 77598. She has lived there with her parents for 10 years. Jenelle pays her parents $150 a month rent. She was born on August 6, 1983. Her Social Security number is 432-87-8976. Her phone number is 802-555-0987.

Jenelle has worked at Center Car Repair for four years. She earns $2,500 a month. That is her only income. The phone number at her job is 802-555-9210. Jenelle has a checking account at First Central Bank. She has no savings account. Jenelle's mother's maiden name is Lee.

Fill out Jenelle's application. Use the facts above.

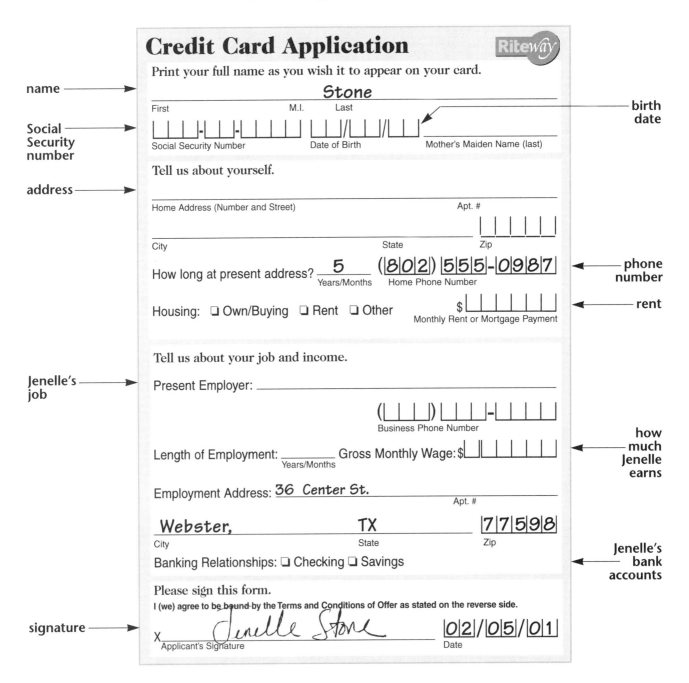

Use the Checklist to make sure you filled out the form correctly.

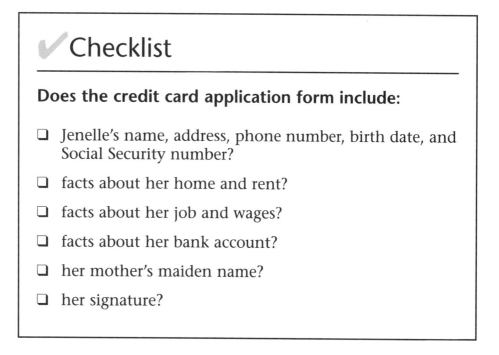

Did you leave any lines on the form blank? If so, go back and fill them in now.

 USE IT   Pretend you are applying for your own credit card. What will you do? Fill out the Credit Card Application, which is Form 12A in *Forms in the Real World*. You can make notes in the space below to help you organize your thoughts. You can make up facts if you do not want to give personal information.

Use the Checklist to make sure your information is complete.
Now fill in the credit card application. Save your completed work in your portfolio.

Lesson 2 Catalog Order Forms

Learning Objective

To buy something from a catalog by filling out an order form

Words to Know

catalog a booklet of items for sale

item number a number that identifies a catalog item

 LEARN IT

Companies that sell things often send **catalogs** to people. You can use the catalogs to shop at home. First, you decide what you want to buy. Then you mail in an order form and a payment. In a few days, the company delivers your order.

When you buy by mail, fill out the order form clearly. Write the **item number** of what you are ordering. This number is shown in the catalog. You must also give details about the item. These include the item's style, color, and size. Then you should tell how many of each item you want. This is called the quantity (Qty.).

List the cost of each item. You may have to add sales tax to the total. There is also a charge for shipping. A chart on the form shows how much to add for that. Then add up the total cost. Use a check or a credit card to pay for the order. If you use a credit card, write the card number and the expiration date, the last date the card can be used. It is printed on the card.

A catalog order form should include:

- your full name and address
- the item number and other details about each item you buy
- the quantity of each item you want
- the total cost of the items with sales tax and shipping
- your credit card's number and expiration date

What kinds of catalogs have you seen? Have you used any of them to shop by mail?

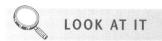

LOOK AT IT

Terri has a catalog from Outdoor Adventures. The company sells camping equipment by mail. The order form from the catalog is shown below. Terri fills it out to order the Sharp Edge backpack.

Terri finds the picture and description of the pack on page 26 of the catalog. She decides to order a red pack. She only wants one pack. The cost is $99.00. Terri decides to pay with her new Riteway credit card. Here is the order form she fills out.

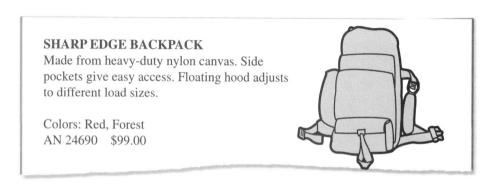

SHARP EDGE BACKPACK
Made from heavy-duty nylon canvas. Side pockets give easy access. Floating hood adjusts to different load sizes.

Colors: Red, Forest
AN 24690 $99.00

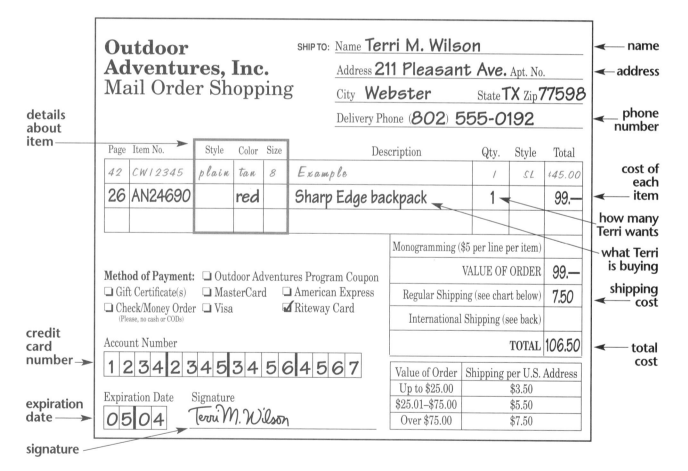

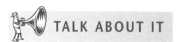

TALK ABOUT IT

What is the item number and color of Terri's backpack? What is the total amount she paid? What is the number of Terri's credit card?

TRY IT

Jenelle wants to order Sharp Edge trail boots on page 37 in the catalog. The catalog entry is shown below. Jenelle wants the black high-cut boots in size 9C. Her last name is Stone. Her address is 678 Hereford Drive, Webster, Texas 77598. Her phone number is 802-555-0987. Jenelle will pay with her Riteway credit card. The number is 3204 4589 3487 0021. The expiration date is 02/04 (February 2004).

Fill in the catalog order form for Jenelle.

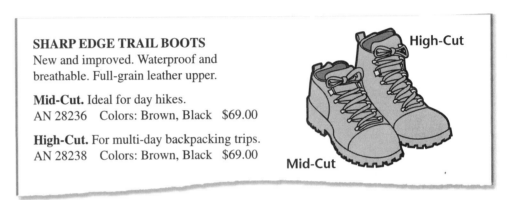

SHARP EDGE TRAIL BOOTS
New and improved. Waterproof and breathable. Full-grain leather upper.

Mid-Cut. Ideal for day hikes.
AN 28236   Colors: Brown, Black $69.00

High-Cut. For multi-day backpacking trips.
AN 28238   Colors: Brown, Black $69.00

High-Cut

Mid-Cut

Outdoor Adventures, Inc.
Mail Order Shopping

SHIP TO: Name **Jenelle Stone**

← name

Address   Apt. No.

City   State   Zip

← address

Delivery Phone (   )

← phone number

details about item →

Page	Item No.	Style	Color	Size	Description	Qty.	Style	Total
42	CW12345	plain	tan	8	Example	1	SL	$45.00

cost of each item ←

how many Jenelle wants

what Jenelle is buying

Method of Payment: ❏ Outdoor Adventures Program Coupon
❏ Gift Certificate(s)   ❏ MasterCard   ❏ American Express
❏ Check/Money Order   ❏ Visa   ☑ Riteway Card
(Please, no cash or CODs)

Monogramming ($5 per line per item)	
VALUE OF ORDER	
Regular Shipping (see chart below)	
International Shipping (see back)	
TOTAL	

shipping cost

total cost

credit card number →

Account Number

expiration date →

Expiration Date   Signature

Value of Order	Shipping per U.S. Address
Up to $25.00	$3.50
$25.01–$75.00	$5.50
Over $75.00	$7.50

signature

Use the Checklist to make sure you filled out the catalog order form correctly.

> ✔ Checklist
>
> ---
>
> **Does your catalog order form include:**
>
> ❑ Jenelle's name and address?
>
> ❑ the item number?
>
> ❑ the size and color of the boots?
>
> ❑ the quantity Jenelle wants?
>
> ❑ the correct total payment?
>
> ❑ Jenelle's credit card information?

Is there anything you should add to the form? If so, go back and add it now.

 USE IT
Pretend you want to order one of the backpacks or a pair of hiking boots from the Outdoor Adventures catalog. Look at Form 13A in *Forms in the Real World*.

You can make notes in the space below to help you organize your thoughts. You can use your own address. Make up any information you need, such as a credit card number.

Use the Checklist to make sure your information is complete.
Now fill in the catalog order form. Save your work in your portfolio.

Lesson 3 Internet Order Forms

Learning Objective

To buy something on the Internet by filling out an order form

Words to Know

Internet a system that links computers all over the world; part of the Internet is called the World Wide Web

Web page a site on the World Wide Web that gives information about someone or something

 LEARN IT

Many stores have **Web pages** on the **Internet.** When you go to a store's Web page, you can click on the item you are shopping for. Pictures and information about the item appear on the screen.

When you click the *Buy* button, a new screen appears. It shows the item you have chosen. At this point, you can click on the color, size, or style you want. When you are finished shopping, a new screen appears. Here you type your name and full mailing address. You might also give your E-mail address.

Reminder

Check the expiration date on your credit card. You cannot use it after the expiration date.

You need a credit card to pay for what you buy on the Internet. You will have to type in your credit card number and expiration date. Next, the amount of your order, plus shipping charges, appears on the screen.

Shopping on the Internet is popular. Because this kind of shopping is so quick and easy, some people get into trouble. They buy things they cannot afford. Think carefully before you click that *Buy* button!

An Internet order form should include:

- information about the items you want to buy
- your name and mailing address
- the number and expiration date of your credit card

Have you ever bought anything on the Internet? If you have, what did you buy? How did you like this kind of shopping?

Terri goes shopping on the Internet. She finds the Camp-Wel Web page. The page lists items for sale. Terri clicks *Sleeping Bags*. She finds a bag she likes, and it is on sale. She clicks on *Buy*. Then she types in the number 1 in the *Qty* (Quantity) box because she only wants one bag.

Next, Terri types her name and address. She also types information about her credit card.

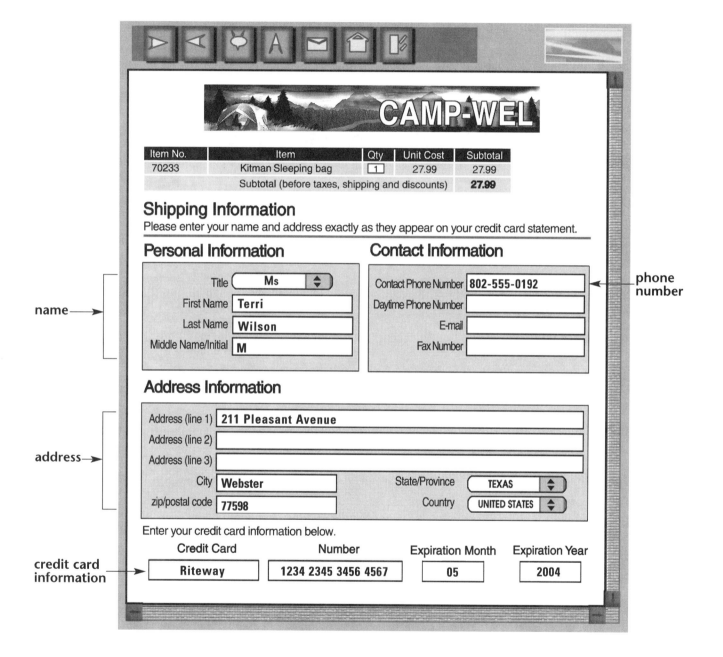

name →

address →

credit card information →

phone number

What kinds of information did Terri type on the Internet order form?

TRY IT

Jenelle wants a sleeping bag like Terri's, so she goes to the Camp-Wel Web page. She clicks on *Sleeping Bags* and finds the same items for sale.

Jenelle's full name is Jenelle Inez Stone. Her address is 678 Hereford Drive, Webster, Texas 77598. Her phone number is 802-555-0987. Her E-mail address is *Star77@hertz.com.* Jenelle has a Riteway credit card. The number is 3204 4589 3487 0021. The expiration date is 2/04 (February 2004).

Fill out the form below for Jenelle. On a computer, you would type in the information. On this page, print it with a pen.

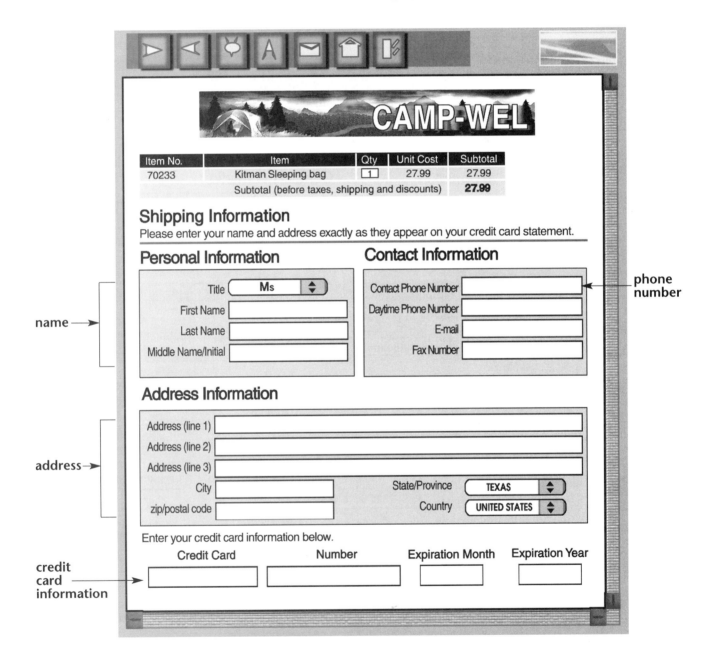

Use the Checklist below. Make sure you filled out the Internet order form correctly.

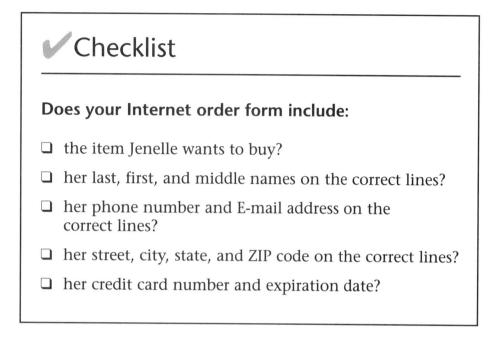

✔ Checklist

Does your Internet order form include:

❑ the item Jenelle wants to buy?

❑ her last, first, and middle names on the correct lines?

❑ her phone number and E-mail address on the correct lines?

❑ her street, city, state, and ZIP code on the correct lines?

❑ her credit card number and expiration date?

Did you fill out the Internet order form correctly? If not, go back and work on it some more.

 USE IT

Imagine you would like to buy something on the Internet. What will you buy? Which Web page will you visit?

In the space below, make notes on the information you will need to type in on the Internet order form. If necessary, make up information you need, such as a credit card number and an expiration date.

Use the Checklist to make sure your information is complete. Now create your own Internet order form on a separate sheet of paper. Then fill it out. If possible, print out an order form from the Internet and fill it in. Save the completed order form in your portfolio.

Lesson 4 Classified Ads

Learning Objective
To sell something by writing a classified ad

Words to Know
classified ads short ads in the newspaper

LEARN IT

The **classified ads** are a popular part of many newspapers. People use these short ads to buy and sell things.

To sell something in the newspaper, write an ad. Begin with a heading that says what you are selling. Next, describe the object. Also tell the price. Finally, tell people how to reach you. Give your phone number and, if you like, your name.

Reminder

You pay for classified ads by the line or by the word. Keep your ad brief and clear.

> ### A classified ad should include:
>
> - a heading that names what you are selling
> - a description of the object and its price
> - your phone number

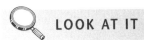
LOOK AT IT

Here is an ad that Jenelle sees in the newspaper:

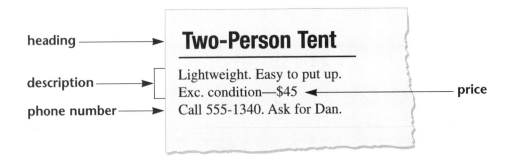

heading ⟶ **Two-Person Tent**

description ⟶ Lightweight. Easy to put up.
Exc. condition—$45 ⟵ price

phone number ⟶ Call 555-1340. Ask for Dan.

TALK ABOUT IT

What details in the ad describe the tent? What do you think the letters *Exc.* mean in the ad? How can Jenelle find out more about the tent?

 **TRY IT**

Jenelle buys the tent from Dan. Because she needs money for her camping trip, she decides to sell some of her own things. Jenelle decides to sell her guitar. It is an acoustic guitar made in Spain. It has a great sound and is in good condition. Jenelle wants to sell it for $50.

In the space below, write a classified ad to sell Jenelle's guitar. Her phone number is 555-0987.

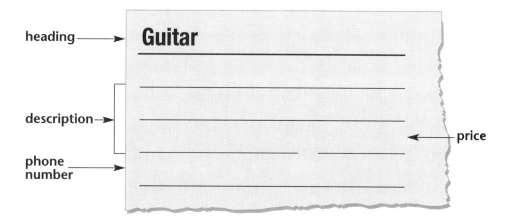

Use the Checklist to see if your classified ad is complete.

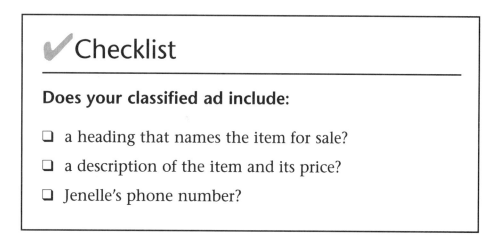

Checklist

Does your classified ad include:

❑ a heading that names the item for sale?

❑ a description of the item and its price?

❑ Jenelle's phone number?

Is your ad complete? If not, go back and work on it some more.

 USE IT

Think of something you would like to sell. What is the best way to try to sell it? Write a classified ad to place in your local newspaper.

Prepare a draft of your ad on a separate sheet of paper. Use the Checklist to make sure your ad is complete.

Now write your final draft on another sheet of paper. Save your classified ad in your portfolio.

Chapter 2

Apply It in the Real World

Camping and Shopping

Jenelle and Terri had a great time camping. In fact, they plan to go again soon. They had some problems with their equipment though. They need more and better equipment. That means more shopping!

Here are some problems they want to solve before their next trip:

1. Jenelle and Terri did not like sleeping in the same tent. Terri decides to sell her two-person tent and buy a one-person tent. Jenelle also wants to buy a one-person tent. Terri wants a stronger tent too. She does not mind if it is a used tent.

2. Finding clean water was a problem on the trip. At home, Jenelle receives the Outdoor Adventures catalog. On page 45, she sees a special water filter for sale. It costs $29 and the item number is TR6721.

3. Jenelle carried pans for cooking on the trip, but they were too big and heavy. When she gets home, Jenelle shops on the Internet. She visits the Camp-Wel site. She sees Cook-Wel cookware on sale for $64.99. Jenelle decides to buy it.

4. Terri did not pay off her credit card bill. Now she is paying high interest on the balance. One day, she sees an ad at the new bank in town. The bank offers a credit card with a lower interest rate. Terri decides to open a new credit card account.

Decide and Write

A. In a small group, talk about Jenelle's and Terri's problems and how to solve them. Think about what forms they need to fill out.

B. Have each group member fill out one of the forms Jenelle and Terri need. You can find the forms in *Forms in the Real World*. Use the information above and in the chapter. When you finish, save your work in your portfolio.

Unit Four

WRAP-UP

In Unit Four, you learned about forms that help you shop and manage money. In Chapter 1, you filled out forms for bank accounts. In Chapter 2, you filled out forms for different kinds of shopping. Knowing how to fill out these forms will help you in the real world.

SHOPPING and MANAGING MONEY

Banking

- Bank Account Applications
- Bank Checks
- Deposits and Withdrawals
- Check Registers

Buying and Selling

- Credit Card Applications
- Catalog Order Forms
- Internet Order Forms
- Classified Ads

Read the types of writing on the chart. Then choose two types of writing. On the lines below, describe a situation from your own life when you could use each type of writing.

1. _____

    _____

2. _____

    _____

What Did You Learn?

On page 106, you listed ways in which writing is useful for banking and shopping. Look again at this list. Can you think of more types of writing to add to the list? What forms might you add?

Unit Five

WRITING at WORK

Work is a big part of everyone's life. At work, you need to communicate with coworkers. Businesses have to keep in touch with other businesses. That is why writing is important in almost every job. The lessons in this unit will help you become a better writer—and a better worker too!

In Unit Five, you will learn about on-the-job writing.

Chapter 1 **Learning Basic Job Skills**

Chapter 2 **Working with Other Businesses**

Chapter 3 **Looking for Jobs**

What Do You Know?

Work with a group of classmates. List different jobs that you have had or seen people do. Then list the types of writing that were part of these jobs. How many different types of writing can you list? Save your lists to use later.

Learning Basic Job Skills

First Day on the Job

It is May 25. For Shawna Robbins, it is a big day. Today is her first day on a new job. She is going to be a receptionist at Century Software. It is a small company, but it is growing fast. It has opened a new office in Chicago. To Shawna, the office seems really busy!

Shawna's boss, Rita Edwards, is friendly. Shawna will work in the office with her. Even so, Shawna is nervous. She wants to do a really good job.

At first, Shawna will be answering the phone and greeting visitors. She will also be sending and receiving faxes. Shawna will have her own computer too. Rita Edwards says Shawna will need to send E-mail messages to different people in the company.

Shawna wants to do a good job at Century Software. She wants to learn the skills she needs to do her job well. She also hopes that this job will lead to a better one someday.

Think About It

Think about these questions and discuss them with a partner. Then share your ideas with the class.

- What types of writing might Shawna do on her new job?

- How might faxes and E-mail messages be used in business?

- What types of writing might you do in most offices?

Lesson 1 Telephone Messages

Learning Objective

To record business telephone calls by completing a message form

Words to Know

telephone message form a printed form used for writing telephone messages

 LEARN IT

Many businesses depend on the telephone. Most businesses give workers pads of **telephone message forms**. Taking good telephone messages helps a business run smoothly.

Always fill out telephone message forms clearly and completely. Make sure you fill in all the information. Write the date and time of each call. Write the name of the person who was called. Write the name of the caller and the business he or she works for. Then write the complete message and your full name as the message taker.

Telephone message forms often have a set of boxes. Next to each box is a short note. These notes list words such as *Telephoned, Called to See You, Please Call,* or *Will Call Again.* When you fill out the form, check the boxes that match the caller's message.

A telephone message should include:

- the date and time of the call
- the name of the person who was called
- the name of the caller and the business
- the caller's phone number
- the message
- the full name of the message taker

Why might telephone messages be important at work? What might happen if you forget to write down part of a message?

 **LOOK AT IT**

As a receptionist at Century Software, Shawna answers phone calls all day. She needs to be able to take clear and complete messages.

At 2:30 P.M. on Monday, Shawna's phone rings. The caller is Edie Gomez. She is a saleswoman at the Chicago office. Ms. Gomez needs some papers sent to her home for a meeting. Tomorrow she will meet with Mr. Liang of the First Central Bank. Ms. Gomez also wants the New York Sales Manager, Don Wrenn, to call her. Ms. Gomez's number is 630-555-2300.

Here is the message form that Shawna fills out:

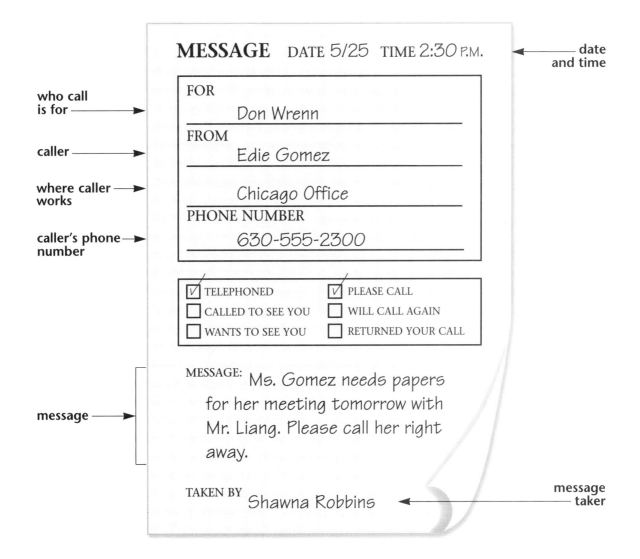

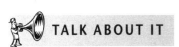 **TALK ABOUT IT**

What information did Shawna include on the message form?
What boxes on the form did she check?

TRY IT

At 3:30 P.M. on Monday, the phone rings at the Chicago office of Century Software. Luis Chavez, the assistant to Edie Gomez, answers the phone. The caller is Don Wrenn, sales manager in New York. He wants to talk to Edie Gomez, who is not at her desk.

Reminder

Make sure you check the correct boxes on the message form.

Mr. Wrenn tells Luis that he is flying into Chicago the next morning. He plans to meet with Ms. Gomez and Mr. Liang. He will be at Ms. Gomez's office at 9:00 A.M. He will bring the papers she needs. Ms. Gomez should call him on his car phone at 212-555-5678. She needs to tell him which papers to bring.

Write the telephone message that Luis should take.

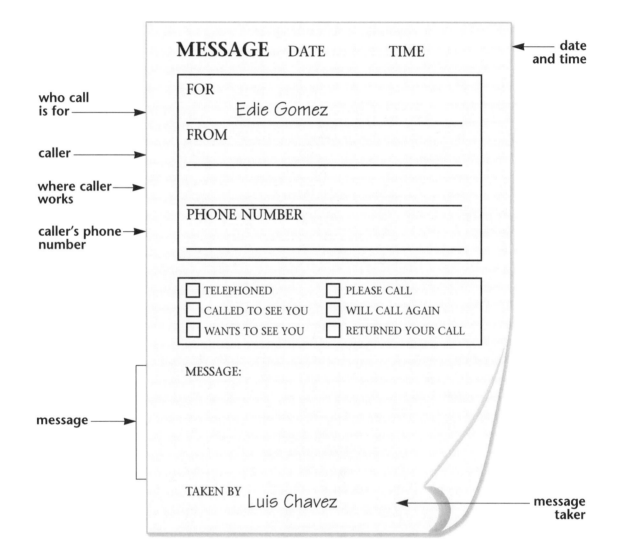

Use the Checklist to see if the telephone message you wrote is clear and complete.

✔ Checklist

Does your telephone message include:

- ❏ the date and time?
- ❏ the person who was called?
- ❏ the caller's name and the name of the business or office location?
- ❏ the caller's phone number?
- ❏ a complete message?
- ❏ the message taker's full name?

Did you leave anything out? Did you check the correct boxes? Go back to the telephone message form. Add anything you need to make it clear and complete.

 USE IT   Imagine you are sitting in for Luis Chavez in the Chicago office of Century Software. You get your first phone call and need to take a message. Read what happens below.

> At 9:00 A.M., you take a phone call for Edie Gomez. The caller is Mr. Liang of the First Central Bank. Ms. Gomez has an appointment with him at 11:00 A.M. that day. Due to an emergency, Mr. Liang has to fly to Denver that day. He wants to cancel the meeting. Ms. Gomez can call his assistant at 606-555-2310. She will set up a new meeting for next week.

Prepare a draft of your phone message on a separate sheet of paper. Use the Checklist above to make sure your message is complete.

Now write your final draft on Form 14A in *Forms in the Real World*. Save your completed message in your portfolio.

Lesson 2 Memos

Learning Objective

To remind someone of something by writing a memo

Word to Know

memo a short message or report to someone

 LEARN IT People who work together must communicate. Memos are a good way to do that. The word **memo** is short for *memorandum*, meaning "reminder." A memo is a short message or report to someone. It might remind all workers to hand in their time sheets, or it might remind one worker of an important meeting.

An office might have pads of memo forms. Most memo forms have a place for the date. The name of the person who will receive the memo goes next to the word *To*. The name of the sender goes next to the word *From*. On the *Subject* line, describe in a few words what the memo is about. Then write the entire message in the space below.

A memo should be clear and complete. Give exact dates, places, and times, if needed. Make sure your readers have all the information they need. A memo should always be typed.

A memo should include:

- the date
- the name(s) of person(s) who will receive the memo
- the name of the sender
- a brief description of what the memo is about
- a clear and complete message

Why might a written memo be more useful than a spoken reminder?

 **LOOK AT IT**

On her first day at work, Rita meets with Shawna and asks her to write a few memos. Shawna uses her boss's name—Rita Edwards—on the *From* line of the memo.

Here is one memo that Shawna types for her boss.

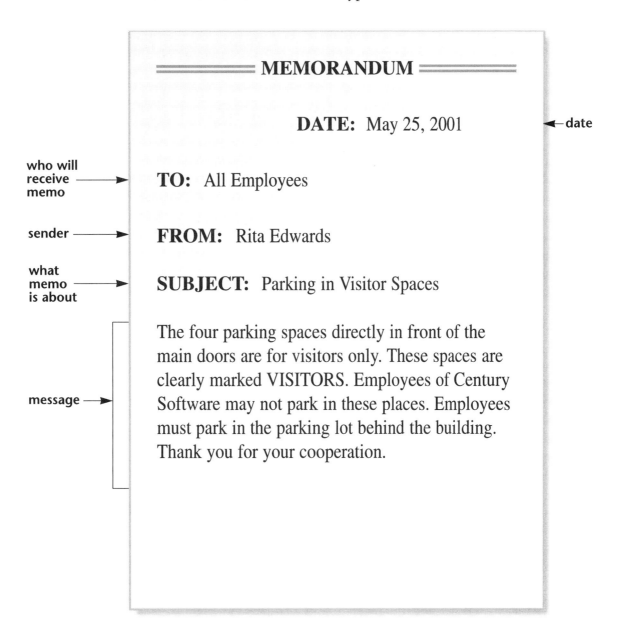

═══ **MEMORANDUM** ═══

DATE: May 25, 2001 ←date

who will receive memo →
TO: All Employees

sender →
FROM: Rita Edwards

what memo is about →
SUBJECT: Parking in Visitor Spaces

message →
The four parking spaces directly in front of the main doors are for visitors only. These spaces are clearly marked VISITORS. Employees of Century Software may not park in these places. Employees must park in the parking lot behind the building. Thank you for your cooperation.

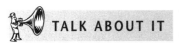 **TALK ABOUT IT**

When did Shawna write this memo? Who received the memo? What did Shawna do to make the memo brief and clear?

 **TRY IT**

Shawna also has to write a memo to Art Godber, Diane Rienzi, and May Chen. They all work in the Accounting Department. She writes the memo on May 25, 2001.

The accounting department is moving from the third floor to the fourth floor. The memo has to remind the workers of this move. The move will happen on the weekend of June 2–3. The memo asks the workers to pack up everything in their offices by 5:00 P.M. on Friday, June 1. The tops of desks and cabinets should be clear. There should be no loose papers or objects.

Write this memo for Shawna. Use the memo form below. Fill in all the lines. Clearly and briefly, write all the information the workers need to know.

=== **MEMORANDUM** ===

DATE: _____ ← date

who will
receive → **TO:** _____
memo

_____

_____

sender → **FROM:** Rita Edwards

what
memo → **SUBJECT:** Accounting Department Move
is about

This is to remind you that the accounting
department will be moving to the fourth floor.

message → _____

_____

_____

_____

Use the Checklist below. Make sure your memo is clear and complete.

✔ Checklist

Does your memo include:

- ❑ the date and time the memo was written?
- ❑ the names of the workers who will receive the memo?
- ❑ the name of the person who sent the memo?
- ❑ a brief description of the subject?
- ❑ where the accounting department is moving?
- ❑ when the move will occur?
- ❑ what the workers must do to get ready for the move?

Is your memo clear and complete? If not, go back and work on it some more.

 USE IT

Imagine you are working at Century Software. Your boss comes to tell you that the company is planning to close early because of a bad storm. How will you let your coworkers know the news? Write a memo explaining that all employees can go home at 2:00 P.M.

Prepare a draft of your memo in the space below or on a separate sheet of paper.

Use the Checklist to make sure your memo is complete. Now write or type your final draft on another sheet of paper. Save the completed memo in your portfolio.

Lesson 3   Fax Cover Sheets

Learning Objective

To prepare to send a fax by completing a fax cover sheet

Words to Know

fax a machine that sends copies of papers over a telephone line; any paper sent by a fax machine

fax cover sheet the first page of a fax

 LEARN IT

Most offices have a fax machine. The machine is plugged into a telephone line. Businesses use fax machines to send copies of papers to one another quickly. A **fax** is any paper that is sent this way.

A worker who sends a fax fills out a **fax cover sheet**, the first page of a fax. The cover sheet names who the fax is for. Because many workers may share one fax machine, this is important. The cover sheet also includes the phone number of the receiver's fax machine. The cover sheet then tells the sender's name and fax number.

Sometimes, a page of a fax is lost while being sent. That is why the cover sheet should tell how many pages there are in the fax. That way, the person who receives the fax will know if it is complete.

A cover sheet has a *Message* box too. You can write a message to the person who will receive your fax. You might explain what you are sending, for example. When you send a fax, be sure to put the cover sheet in the fax machine first.

A fax cover sheet should include:

- the name and fax number of the person receiving the fax
- the name and fax number of the sender
- the number of pages in the fax
- a short message

Have you ever sent a fax? Have you ever received one? When might a fax machine come in handy?

Just before noon, Rita Edwards asks Shawna to send a fax to Del Daily. He is a salesperson for Century Software. Mr. Daily's fax number is 516-555-9087. The fax is 8 pages long, plus the cover sheet. The pages give information about a new software program called "Theta 7." Mr. Daily asked for this information a week ago.

Shawna finds a blank fax cover sheet in her desk. She fills it out. Then she sends the fax and cover sheet to Mr. Daily.

Here is the fax cover sheet that Shawna fills out. Note that the abbreviation *No.* means "number."

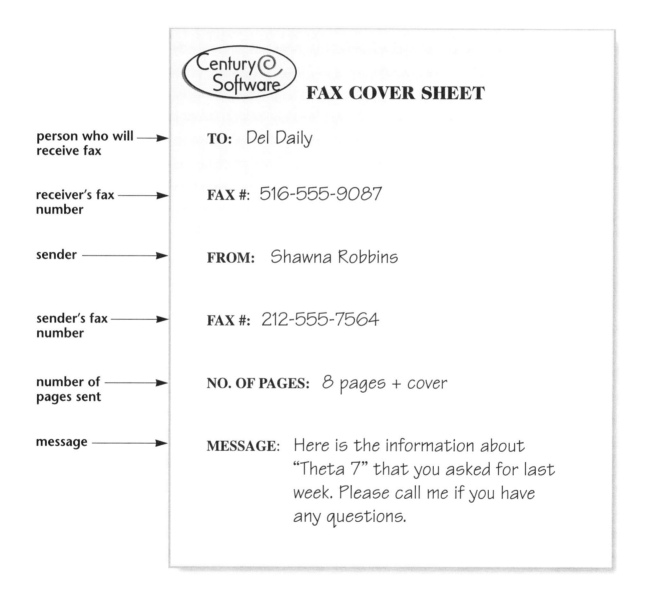

Century Software **FAX COVER SHEET**

person who will receive fax →
TO: Del Daily

receiver's fax number →
FAX #: 516-555-9087

sender →
FROM: Shawna Robbins

sender's fax number →
FAX #: 212-555-7564

number of pages sent →
NO. OF PAGES: 8 pages + cover

message →
MESSAGE: Here is the information about "Theta 7" that you asked for last week. Please call me if you have any questions.

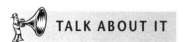
TALK ABOUT IT

How many pages did Shawna fax to Mr. Daily? What fax number did Shawna dial to send the fax?

On Monday afternoon, Shawna sends a fax to Edie Gomez. Ms. Gomez works in the company's Chicago office. Her fax number is 630-555-0908. The fax is a copy of the Mays contract. Ms. Gomez wants to review it again. The fax is 9 pages long, plus the cover sheet. Ms. Gomez asked for a copy of the contract on May 22, three days earlier. Shawna's fax number is 212-555-7564.

Use the information above to complete this fax cover sheet.

Century Software FAX COVER SHEET

person who will receive fax → **TO:** _____

receiver's fax number → **FAX #:** _____

sender → **FROM:** Shawna Robbins

sender's fax number → **FAX #:** 212-555-7564

number of pages sent → **NO. OF PAGES:** _____

message → **MESSAGE:** _____

_____

_____

_____

_____

Use the Checklist to see if the fax cover sheet is clear and complete.

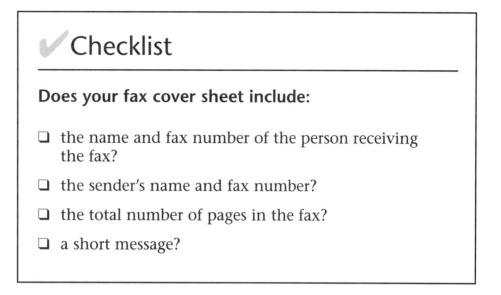

✔ Checklist

Does your fax cover sheet include:

❑ the name and fax number of the person receiving the fax?

❑ the sender's name and fax number?

❑ the total number of pages in the fax?

❑ a short message?

Did you leave anything out of the fax cover sheet? Go back to the form. Add anything you need to make it clear and complete.

 USE IT

Shawna Robbins is on her coffee break, and you are sitting in for her again. The phone rings and you answer it. Read what happens below.

It is Don Wrenn. He wants you to fax him copies of three letters from Mr. Liang. The letters are on his desk. Mr. Wrenn gives you his fax number at home 212-555-8204. He wants the fax right away.

You go to Mr. Wrenn's desk. You only find two letters from Mr. Liang there. One letter is 2 pages. The other is 3 pages. You prepare to send the fax. The fax is 5 pages long, plus the cover sheet. On the cover sheet, you will need to write a message. Tell Mr. Wrenn that there were only two letters on his desk.

Make notes for your fax cover sheet in the space below.

Use the Checklist to make sure your cover sheet is complete. Now write the final draft of your fax cover sheet on another sheet of paper. Save your work in your portfolio.

Lesson 4 E-mail Messages

Learning Objective

To send a message by writing an E-mail

Word to Know

subject topic of an E-mail message stated in a few words

 LEARN IT

Many workers use computers. Often, computers in businesses are linked by telephone lines. This lets workers send and receive E-mail messages. Workers send E-mail messages to coworkers or people in other companies.

To write an E-mail message, sign on and click the screen to create a message. This screen has several sections. Use the Tab key to move between them. In the *To* box, type the E-mail address of the person to whom you are writing.

You should also fill in the *Subject* box of the screen. Write a few words about the **subject**, or topic, of your message. In the *Message* box, type the message itself. Last, type your name. When you have finished your message, click the *Send* button.

An E-mail message should include:

- the E-mail address of the person you are writing to
- the subject of the E-mail
- the E-mail message itself
- the name of the sender

Why do you think E-mail can be useful to a company?

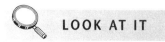

LOOK AT IT

On her first day at Century Software, Shawna learns how to send and receive E-mail. Her E-mail address is *shawnarobbins@csi.com.* Later in the day, Shawna gets an E-mail from Edna Glick in the Human Resources office.

Here is the E-mail that Shawna receives:

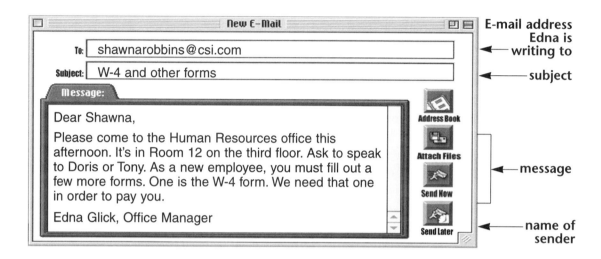

When Shawna gets the E-mail message, she clicks the *Reply* button. She writes this short E-mail reply back to Ms. Glick.

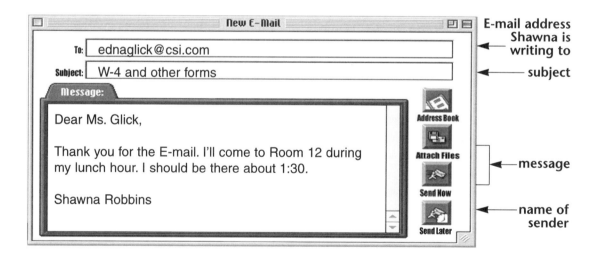

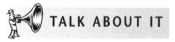

TALK ABOUT IT

What is Shawna's E-mail address? What is Edna Glick's E-mail address? What message does Edna send to Shawna? What answer does Shawna send to Edna?

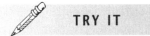

TRY IT

On Monday afternoon, Rita Edwards asks Shawna to send an E-mail to Edie Gomez. Ms. Gomez's E-mail address is *ediegomez@csi.com.* Ms. Edwards wants Ms. Gomez to send in a copy of her April sales report. This report is a month late.

Because you are not at a computer right now, print the E-mail message that Shawna might send to Ms. Gomez. Fill in each box.

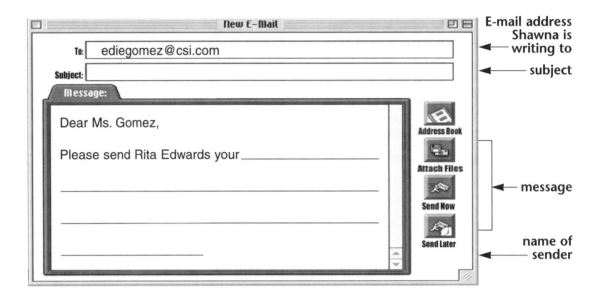

Edie Gomez sends back an E-mail message to Shawna right away. Edie says that she did send in the April sales report two weeks ago. She wonders if it is in Ms. Edwards's office somewhere.

In the box below, print Edie's E-mail message to Shawna.

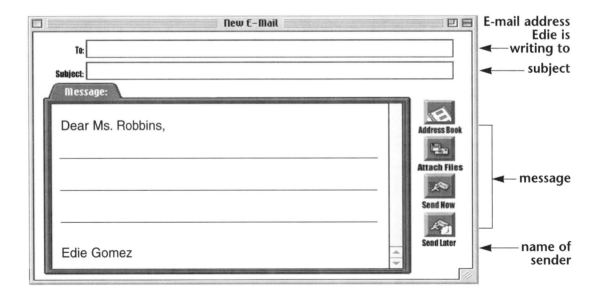

Use the Checklist to see if the E-mail messages you printed are clear and complete.

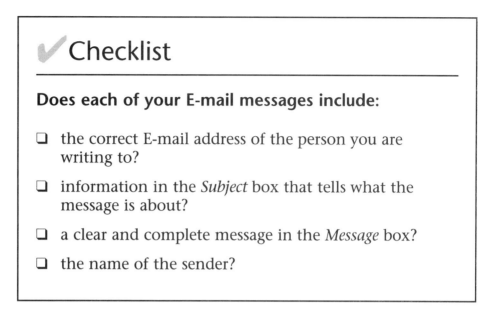

✔ Checklist

Does each of your E-mail messages include:

❑ the correct E-mail address of the person you are writing to?

❑ information in the *Subject* box that tells what the message is about?

❑ a clear and complete message in the *Message* box?

❑ the name of the sender?

Did you leave anything out of your E-mail messages? If so, go back to them now. Add anything you need to make them clear and complete.

USE IT

Imagine that you are working at Century Software. Read what happens below.

> You need to send an E-mail message to Shawna. You want to schedule a meeting with her next week to talk about your work schedules. You have an important training session next week. You will not be able to sit in for her during her lunch hour next Thursday or Friday. Shawna's E-mail address is *shawnarobbins@csi.com.*

Prepare a draft of your E-mail in the space below or on the computer.

Use the Checklist to make sure your message is complete. Now write your final draft on a separate sheet or on the computer. Save (or print out and save) your E-mail message in your portfolio.

Apply It in the Real World

The Second Day on the Job

Imagine that you are working with Shawna. It is May 26, 2001, Shawna's second day on the job. During the day, there is a lot to do.

Here are Shawna's tasks that include writing:

1. Shawna gets an E-mail message from Tony Basso. His E-mail address is *tonybasso@csi.com.* He works in the Human Resources office. He writes that Shawna forgot to sign her W-4 form. Could she please come to his office and sign it?

2. Shawna answers the phone. It is Larry Rivera from the Chicago office. The call is for Bill Jeffers, who is out of the office. Bill should call Larry at 630-555-0631. Larry wants to meet with Bill this week.

3. Rita Edwards asks Shawna to send a memo to the sales department. Rita wants to tell the people in sales that monthly sales reports have been late. The reports must arrive by the fifth of every month. May sales reports are due on June 5.

4. Don Wrenn calls Shawna from the Chicago office. He needs copies of three letters that he wrote to Ben Nakamura. Shawna should send the copies to Don in Chicago. His fax number is 630-555-8902. Shawna's fax number is 212-555-7564.

Decide and Write

A. In a small group, talk about each task. Decide which type of writing Shawna needs in each situation. Remember what you have learned about each type.

B. Now have each group member create one piece of writing Shawna needs. Use a form in *Forms in the Real World* if you wish. Save your work in your portfolio.

Working with Other Businesses

A Day at Sunshine Fruit and Nut

It was a bad day at The Sunshine Fruit and Nut Company.

First, the company ran out of peanuts for its granola bars. Workers stood around doing nothing. One of the supervisors thought he had ordered peanuts. He was not sure though.

To make things worse, the Health Department checked one of Sunshine's factories. The inspectors did not like what they found. Sunshine has to clean up its mixing area fast!

There is another problem too. The company has a new packing machine that does not work right. Sometimes, it does not seal the bags of granola. Other times, it tears the bags. The company must do something about the machine.

Finally, there are money problems. Some stores are not paying Sunshine on time. The company needs those payments right away.

Think About It

Think about these questions and discuss them with a partner. Then share your ideas with the class.

• What problems does The Sunshine Fruit and Nut Company have?

• How might writing letters help the company solve its problems?

• Why is solving problems important in a successful business?

Lesson 1 Purchase Order Forms

Learning Objective

To purchase something for a company by filling out a purchase order form

Words to Know

purchase something a company buys

purchase order form a form to keep track of purchases

vendor a person or company that sells something to a business

 LEARN IT

Businesses buy many things. They buy desks and computers. They buy cars and machines. They buy materials to make things. Businesses must keep track of their **purchases**. To order something, a worker fills out a **purchase order form**. The worker's boss signs the form. Then the company makes the purchase. Each purchase order has its own number.

To fill out a purchase order form, first write the date and your name. Then write the name and address of the **vendor**, or seller. Describe what you want to buy. Tell how many of each item you are ordering. This is the *quantity*. Then tell what *units* the company uses to measure amounts: boxes, cases, bags, and so on. Write how much each unit costs. This is the *unit price*. Then multiply the quantity by the unit price. Finally, add up the total cost of the purchase.

A purchase order form should include:

- the name and address of the vendor
- the date of the purchase
- the name of the worker who is ordering
- item number, units, unit price, and total cost
- the signature of someone who can approve the order

Think of a business you know about. What things might this business need to buy?

LOOK AT IT

Here is a purchase order form that Manny Jones fills out. The name and address of The Sunshine Fruit and Nut Company are printed at the top. Manny sends a copy of the form to the Top Notch Nut Company, the vendor.

As you can see, Manny is ordering peanuts. He fills in the item number—76578—from the vendor's catalog. In all, he wants 10 cases. Each case costs $80. The total cost of the peanuts is $800. Manny is also ordering hazelnuts. He fills in the item number—27412. He wants 6 cases. Each case costs $50. The total cost of the hazelnuts is $300. The total cost of both items is $1,100. Randi Isolo signs the form. She is the vice president of The Sunshine Fruit and Nut Company. By signing, she approves the purchase.

seller's name and address

item numbers

what Manny is ordering

signature of person who approves order

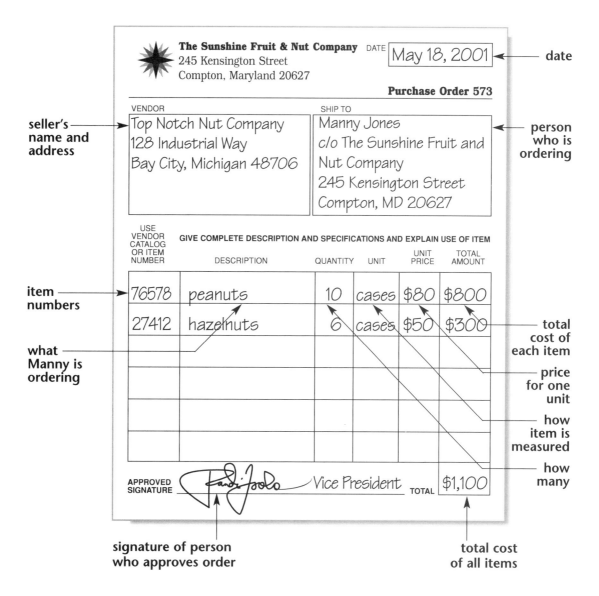

date

person who is ordering

total cost of each item

price for one unit

how item is measured

how many

total cost of all items

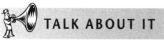

TALK ABOUT IT

What did Manny purchase besides peanuts? How much of this item did he buy? How did Manny figure out the total cost of the order?

TRY IT

The Sunshine Fruit and Nut Company buys from many vendors. Manny has to fill out another purchase order for nuts the same day. The National Nut Company is the vendor.

Manny needs 20 cases of almonds. The item number is 2341 in the vendor's catalog. Each case costs $150.

Manny also needs cases of pecans. The item number is 2381. Each case costs $130. Manny orders 10 cases. Manny orders the almonds and pecans on the same order form.

Fill out the purchase order form for the nuts. Show the item number, quantity, unit, unit price, and cost of each type of nut. Then show the total cost of the order.

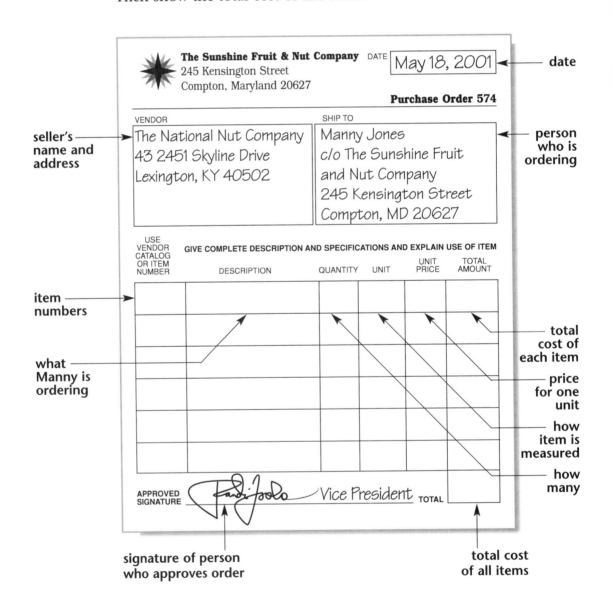

seller's name and address

item numbers

what Manny is ordering

signature of person who approves order

date

person who is ordering

total cost of each item

price for one unit

how item is measured

how many

total cost of all items

Use the Checklist to see if your purchase order form is complete.

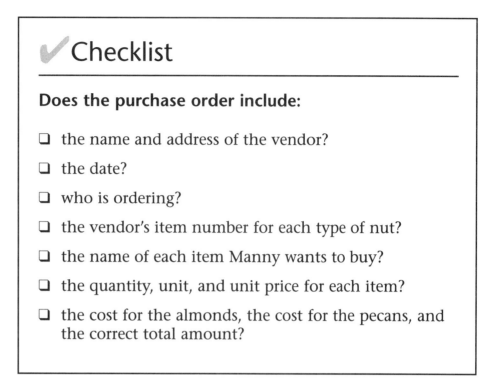

✔ Checklist

Does the purchase order include:

❏ the name and address of the vendor?

❏ the date?

❏ who is ordering?

❏ the vendor's item number for each type of nut?

❏ the name of each item Manny wants to buy?

❏ the quantity, unit, and unit price for each item?

❏ the cost for the almonds, the cost for the pecans, and the correct total amount?

Did you fill in the purchase order form completely? If not, go back and make it complete now.

 USE IT

Imagine that you have started your own company. What kind of company is it? Think of some things you might need to buy. Who will be the vendor? Make up a vendor name and any other information you need.

Look at Form 15A in *Forms in the Real World*. You can make notes in the space below to help you organize your thoughts.

Use the Checklist to make sure your information is complete. Now fill in the Purchase Order Form. Save your completed form in your portfolio.

Lesson 2 Letters of Request

Learning Objective

To ask for something by writing a letter of request

Words to Know

letter of request a business letter that asks for something

modified-block style a way of typing a business letter

 LEARN IT

Office workers write many **letters of request.** These letters often ask for information.

When you are writing a letter of request, say exactly what you want. Give a reason for your request. Be polite. Then your reader will be more likely to do what you ask.

Like other business letters, letters of request have six parts. These are the heading, inside address, greeting, body, closing, and signature.

The **modified-block style** is one way to type a business letter. The heading is on the right side. So are the closing and the signature. The inside address is on the left side. Each paragraph is indented.

A letter of request should include:

- the six parts of a business letter: heading, inside address, greeting, body, closing, and signature
- exactly what you want and why you want it
- polite language

A modified-block style business letter should include:

- the heading, closing, and signature on the right
- the inside address and greeting on the left
- indented paragraphs in the body

Why is it important to use polite language in a letter of request?

The Sunshine Fruit and Nut Company is having trouble with a new machine. This machine places nuts in bags. Sometimes, the machine tears the bags. At other times, it does not seal them. Anwar Houmeni is the factory manager. He wants to solve these problems. Last week, he met someone who uses the same machine in another company. That gave him an idea. So he writes a letter of request.

Notice that the business letter is typed in modified-block style.

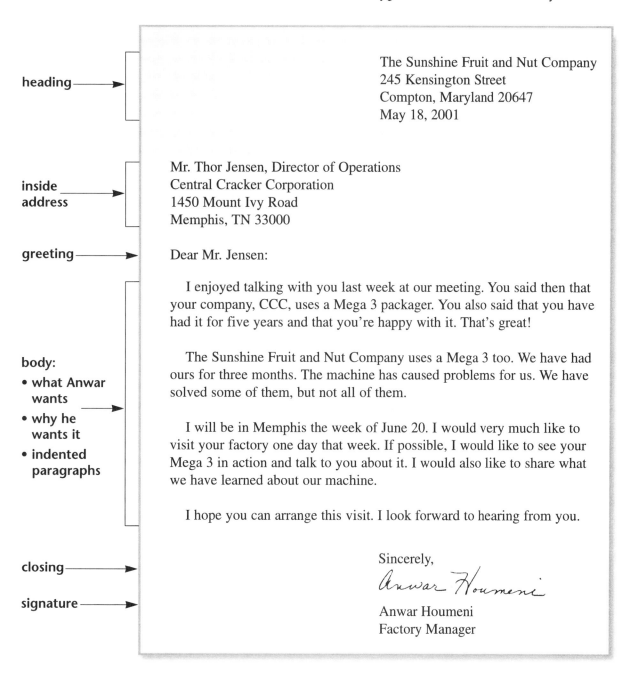

heading →

The Sunshine Fruit and Nut Company
245 Kensington Street
Compton, Maryland 20647
May 18, 2001

inside address →

Mr. Thor Jensen, Director of Operations
Central Cracker Corporation
1450 Mount Ivy Road
Memphis, TN 33000

greeting →

Dear Mr. Jensen:

body:
• what Anwar wants
• why he wants it
• indented paragraphs

I enjoyed talking with you last week at our meeting. You said then that your company, CCC, uses a Mega 3 packager. You also said that you have had it for five years and that you're happy with it. That's great!

The Sunshine Fruit and Nut Company uses a Mega 3 too. We have had ours for three months. The machine has caused problems for us. We have solved some of them, but not all of them.

I will be in Memphis the week of June 20. I would very much like to visit your factory one day that week. If possible, I would like to see your Mega 3 in action and talk to you about it. I would also like to share what we have learned about our machine.

I hope you can arrange this visit. I look forward to hearing from you.

closing →
signature →

Sincerely,

Anwar Houmeni

Anwar Houmeni
Factory Manager

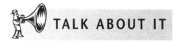

TALK ABOUT IT What request did Anwar make? Did he give a reason for the request? Would you say the letter is polite? Why?

TRY IT

Sunshine products are not selling as well as they have in the past. No one knows why. Vice President Randi Isolo has to do something. Two years ago, Sunshine's best salesperson retired. For years, Maria Falcone led the company in sales. Randi Isolo writes to Ms. Falcone. In her letter, Ms. Isolo asks Ms. Falcone to come to the company's Maryland office on July 1 or 2. She wants Ms. Falcone to speak to the Sunshine sales force about sales methods that made her successful.

Write this letter of request for Randi Isolo in the modified-block style. The heading is The Sunshine Fruit and Nut Company, 245 Kensington Street, Compton, Maryland 20647. Maria Falcone's address is 111 St. Peter's Way, Columbia, South Carolina 29261.

heading →

The Sunshine Fruit and Nut Company

_____

_____

May 22, 2001

inside address →

_____

_____

_____

greeting →

Dear Ms. Falcone:

    I hope you are enjoying your well-earned retirement. We really miss you here at Sunshine. _____

_____

_____

_____

_____

_____

_____

body:
- what Ms. Isolo wants
- why she wants it
- indented paragraphs

                Sincerely,

closing →

signature →

Randi Isolo
Vice President

Use the Checklist to make sure your letter of request is complete.

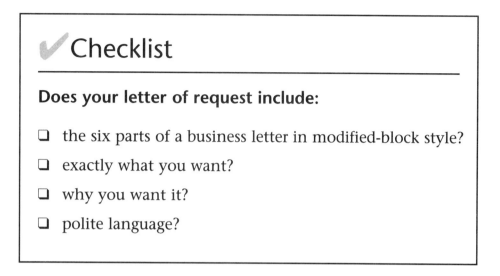

✔ Checklist

Does your letter of request include:

❑ the six parts of a business letter in modified-block style?

❑ exactly what you want?

❑ why you want it?

❑ polite language?

Is your letter clear and complete? If not, go back and work on it some more.

 USE IT Write a letter of request to a business that sells something you want to buy. In your letter, ask for a catalog or some other information about the item that interests you. Explain that you need this information to help you decide whether to buy the item.

Prepare a draft of your letter of request in the space below.

Use the Checklist to make sure your letter is complete. Now write or type your final draft on a separate sheet of paper. Save your letter in your portfolio.

Lesson 3 Letters of Complaint

Learning Objective

To try to solve a problem by writing a letter of complaint

Words to Know

letter of complaint a business letter that asks someone to solve a problem

 LEARN IT

In any business, there are problems. A worker may not do a good job. Companies may not pay their bills. Buyers may not be happy with things they have ordered. To deal with problems, people write **letters of complaint**.

A letter of complaint should be clear and direct. It must say exactly what is wrong. The writer should include details. That way, the reader will understand the problem. The writer should also suggest a fair way to solve the problem.

Do not show anger in a letter of complaint. Angry feelings might make the problem harder to solve. Use polite yet firm language. Your reader will then be more likely to help you.

A letter of complaint should include:

- exactly what the problem is
- an idea for solving the problem fairly
- polite yet firm language

Why might a business send a letter of complaint?

The State Health Department checks one of The Sunshine Fruit and Nut Company factories. The inspectors find that the mixing area is very dirty. Sidney Hoffman is in charge of this factory.

Randi Isolo, the vice president, writes a letter of complaint to Sidney Hoffman. Ms. Isolo describes the problem. She also suggests a way to solve it.

Here is the letter that Ms. Isolo sends to Sidney Hoffman.

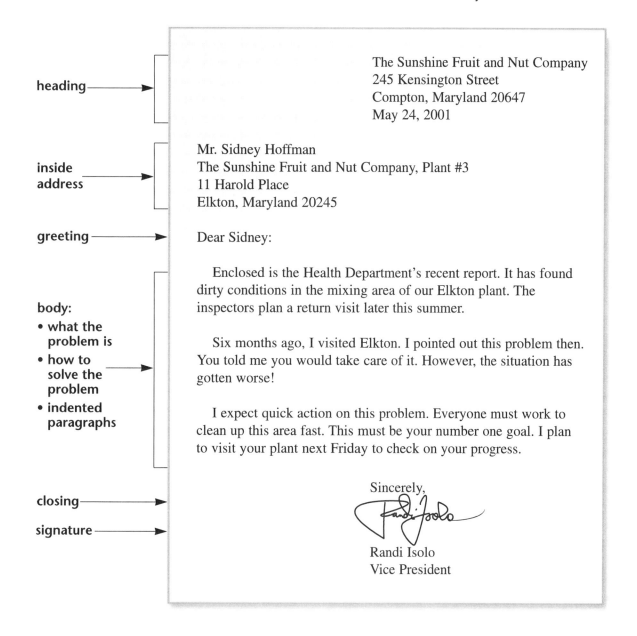

heading

The Sunshine Fruit and Nut Company
245 Kensington Street
Compton, Maryland 20647
May 24, 2001

inside address

Mr. Sidney Hoffman
The Sunshine Fruit and Nut Company, Plant #3
11 Harold Place
Elkton, Maryland 20245

greeting

Dear Sidney:

body:
- **what the problem is**
- **how to solve the problem**
- **indented paragraphs**

Enclosed is the Health Department's recent report. It has found dirty conditions in the mixing area of our Elkton plant. The inspectors plan a return visit later this summer.

Six months ago, I visited Elkton. I pointed out this problem then. You told me you would take care of it. However, the situation has gotten worse!

I expect quick action on this problem. Everyone must work to clean up this area fast. This must be your number one goal. I plan to visit your plant next Friday to check on your progress.

Sincerely,

Randi Isolo
Vice President

closing

signature

TALK ABOUT IT What problem does the letter describe? How does Ms. Isolo think Sidney Hoffman can solve the problem?

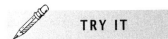 **TRY IT**

Manny Jones is not happy. A few weeks ago he ordered pecans and almonds. The National Nut Company shipped his order. When workers opened the nuts, some of the nuts were moldy.

Manny writes a letter of complaint to Steve Forest, vice president of The National Nut Company. He asks Mr. Forest to send him three new cases of pecans and two new cases of almonds. He wants these nuts free of charge.

Write Manny's letter of complaint. The heading is The Sunshine Fruit and Nut Company, 245 Kensington Street, Compton, Maryland 20647. The date is June 15, 2001. The National Nut Company's address is 432451 Skyline Drive, Lexington, Kentucky 40502.

heading →

The Sunshine Fruit and Nut Company

_____

_____

June 15, 2001

**inside
address** →

Mr. Steve Forest, Vice President
The National Nut Company

_____

_____

greeting →

_____ :

body:
- **what the
  problem is**
- **how to solve
  the problem**
- **indented
  paragraphs**

Recently, we received an order of nuts from The National Nut

Company. The nuts were clearly not fresh. _____

_____

_____

_____

_____

closing →

signature →

_____

Manny Jones

Manny Jones
Production Manager

Use the Checklist to make sure your letter of complaint is complete.

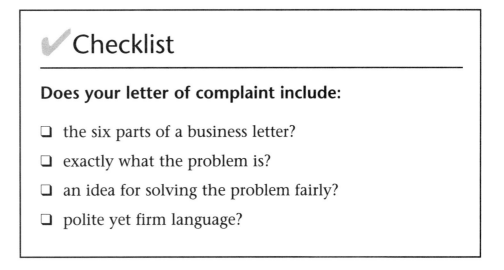

✔ Checklist

Does your letter of complaint include:

❑ the six parts of a business letter?

❑ exactly what the problem is?

❑ an idea for solving the problem fairly?

❑ polite yet firm language?

Is your letter of complaint clear and complete? If not, go back and work on it some more.

USE IT

Pretend that you are one of the workers at The Sunshine Fruit and Nut Company. Imagine that you are unhappy with something you have bought for the company. Write a letter of complaint. Describe the problem. Then suggest a fair way to solve it.

Prepare a draft of your letter in the space below.

Reminder

Use polite yet firm language in your letter of complaint.

Use the Checklist to make sure your letter is complete. Now write or type your letter of complaint on a separate sheet of paper. Save the letter in your portfolio.

Lesson 4 Follow-up Letters

Learning Objective

To remind someone that you need something by writing a follow-up letter

Words to Know

follow-up letter a business letter that reminds the reader of a request or complaint

full-block style a way of typing a business letter

 LEARN IT

Sometimes you may not receive an answer to your letter of request or complaint. Sometimes you may receive an answer that you do not like. At these times, you will need to write a **follow-up letter**.

A follow-up letter reminds the reader that you need something done. It mentions the first letter you wrote. It should also mention any answer you received. Give all the important facts. Say exactly what you want now. Be brief.

You can type a business letter in modified-block style or **full-block** style. In full-block style, all six parts of the letter are at the left margin. You do not indent the paragraphs. Some companies like the modified-block style. Others choose the full-block style. Both are correct.

> **Reminder**
>
> In the modified-block style, the heading, closing, and signature are on the right side. The inside address is on the left. Each paragraph is indented.

A follow-up letter should include:

- the date of the first letter you sent and any answer you have received

- all important facts

- what you want now

A business letter in full-block style should include:

- all six parts of the letter at the left side of the page

- no indented paragraphs

When might a business send a follow-up letter?

Price Rite Foods has not paid its bill in four months. The company owes Sunshine Fruit and Nut a lot of money. Audrey Dixon at Sunshine wrote to Price Rite last month. The company did not answer her letter, so she writes a follow-up letter.

Audrey typed the letter in the full-block style.

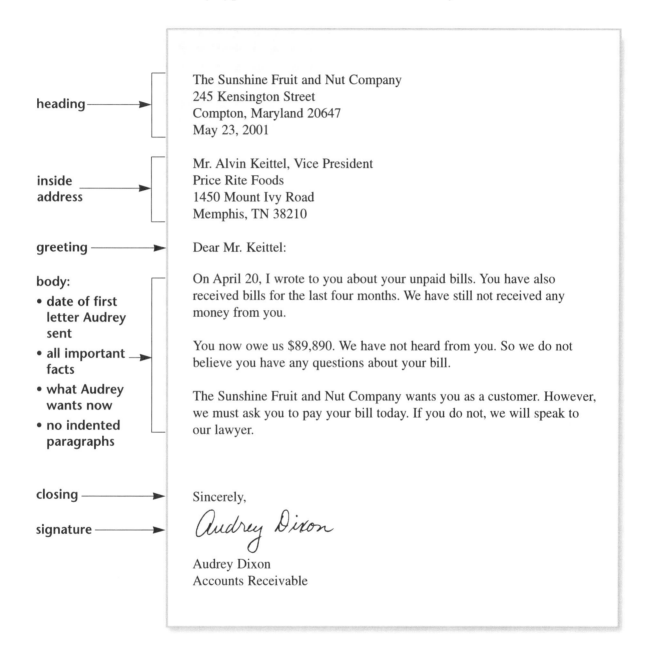

heading →

The Sunshine Fruit and Nut Company
245 Kensington Street
Compton, Maryland 20647
May 23, 2001

inside address →

Mr. Alvin Keittel, Vice President
Price Rite Foods
1450 Mount Ivy Road
Memphis, TN 38210

greeting →

Dear Mr. Keittel:

body:
• date of first letter Audrey sent
• all important facts →
• what Audrey wants now
• no indented paragraphs

On April 20, I wrote to you about your unpaid bills. You have also received bills for the last four months. We have still not received any money from you.

You now owe us $89,890. We have not heard from you. So we do not believe you have any questions about your bill.

The Sunshine Fruit and Nut Company wants you as a customer. However, we must ask you to pay your bill today. If you do not, we will speak to our lawyer.

closing →

Sincerely,

signature →

Audrey Dixon

Audrey Dixon
Accounts Receivable

TALK ABOUT IT

What was the date of Audrey's first letter? What is the date of the follow-up letter? What does Audrey want Alvin Keittel to do?

TRY IT

On May 25, Manny Jones wrote to the vice president of The National Nut Company about a shipment of moldy nuts. He asked the company to replace three cases of pecans and two cases of almonds.

Manny received no answer to his letter. On July 15, he writes a follow-up letter to the vice president, Steve Forest. Manny demands that National Nut replace the moldy nuts. He says Sunshine Fruit and Nut will not buy from National Nut again unless Mr. Forest solves the problem.

Write the follow-up letter for Manny. Use the full-block style.

heading

The Sunshine Fruit and Nut Company

_____

_____

July 15, 2001

inside address

Mr. Steve Forest, Vice President

_____

432451 Skyline Dr.
Lexington, KY 40502

greeting

_____

body:
- date of first letter Manny sent
- all important facts
- what he wants now
- no indented paragraphs

On June 1, I wrote to you about a shipment of moldy nuts we received from

your company. _____

_____

_____

_____

closing

_____

signature

Manny Jones

Manny Jones
Production Manager

Use the Checklist below. Make sure your follow-up letter is clear and complete.

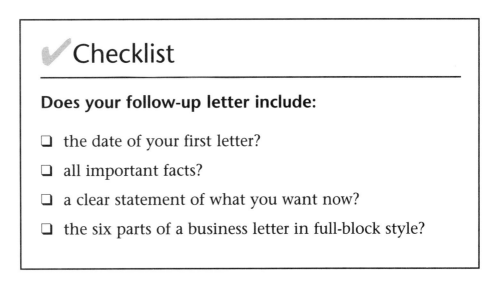

✔ Checklist

Does your follow-up letter include:

❏ the date of your first letter?

❏ all important facts?

❏ a clear statement of what you want now?

❏ the six parts of a business letter in full-block style?

Is your follow-up letter clear and complete? If not, go back and work on it some more.

 USE IT   Look again at the letters of request and complaint that you wrote in Lessons 2 and 3 in this chapter. Imagine that you have received no answers to these letters. Write a follow-up to one of the letters.

Prepare a draft of your letter in the space below or on a separate sheet of paper.

Use the Checklist to make sure your letter is complete. Now write or type your follow-up letter on another sheet of paper. Save your letter in your portfolio.

Chapter 2

Apply It in the Real World

Another Day at Sunshine Fruit and Nut

Imagine that you and three classmates run The Sunshine Fruit and Nut Company. On June 1, 2001, you are having your daily meeting.

There are four problems you need to solve:

1. Sidney Hoffman, Sunshine's manager, wants to replace the company's mixers. Sidney has heard about a company called Modern Machinery. The address is 150 Center Avenue, Sparks, Iowa 53172. Modern makes mixing machines. Modern's president is Ben Segal.

2. On May 18, Anwar Houmeni wrote to Thor Jensen. Thor works at the Central Cracker Company. Anwar wanted to visit Thor's factory and to ask some questions about a Mega 3 food packager. However, Thor has not answered Anwar's letter. Anwar really wants to visit the cracker company in Memphis in late June.

3. The dried apples from American Apples were late in May. The apples were supposed to arrive at Sunshine on May 1. They did not arrive until May 13. The company's president is Susan Day. Her address is 375 Main Street, Clinton, Maryland 20773.

4. Jane Williams at Sunshine needs ten cases of Brazil nuts from Top Notch Nut Company. The item number is 34132. The unit price is $50.

Decide and Write

A. In a small group, talk about each problem. Decide which letter or form you need to solve each problem. Think about what you might write in the letters.

B. Now have each group member write one of the letters or forms you need. You may need to look at the lessons in this chapter for addresses or other details. Use a form in *Forms in the Real World* if you choose. Save your work in your portfolio.

Chapter 3

Looking for Jobs

Job Wanted!

Looking for a job is part of life. Everyone does it sooner or later. Most people look for jobs many times in their lives.

Right now, Danny Ortega is looking for a job. His last job was at a computer store. The store closed. Danny hopes he can find another job working with computers.

Writing is part of most job searches. That surprised Danny. For example, he learned that he had to write a résumé. A résumé lists information about Danny—his education and jobs. Danny also has to write letters to ask about jobs. They are called letters of application. Danny has filled out job applications too.

So far, Danny has had two job interviews. He has not gotten any job offers though. Finding a job can take time. Danny is still hopeful. He knows the right job is out there. He just has to find it!

Think About It

Think about these questions and discuss them with a partner. Then share your ideas with the class.

- Suppose you had to find a job. How would you look for one?

- What types of writing might you do to find this job?

- What is a job interview? How might you get one?

Lesson 1 Résumés

Learning Objective

To tell about your education and experience by writing a résumé

Words to Know

résumé a summary of a person's education and work experience

references people who can give information about someone else

  LEARN IT

A **résumé** lists details about a person. It shows where the person went to school. It tells the jobs he or she has had. A résumé helps an employer who wants to hire someone. It also helps the person tell about why he or she could do a job well.

Type your name, address, and phone number at the top of your résumé. List details about your education and jobs. List volunteer work too. It is important to show how much you have done.

Your résumé should be typed neatly. Type categories, such as *Education* and *Work Experience* on the left. Type details for each category on the right. List your most recent job first.

References are people who can give information about you. Type their names on your résumé, or type *Available upon request*. That means you will give their names later if they are needed. Be sure to ask people before you use their name as a reference.

A résumé should include:

- your name, address, and phone number at the top

- details about your education

- details about jobs or activities you have done and your work skills

- the names of references or a statement about them

What would an employer learn by looking at a person's résumé?

LOOK AT IT Danny Ortega centers his full name, address, and phone number at the top of his résumé. He types the categories *Education* and *Work Experience* on the left. Then he types details about his education and jobs on the right. He lists dates for each job too.

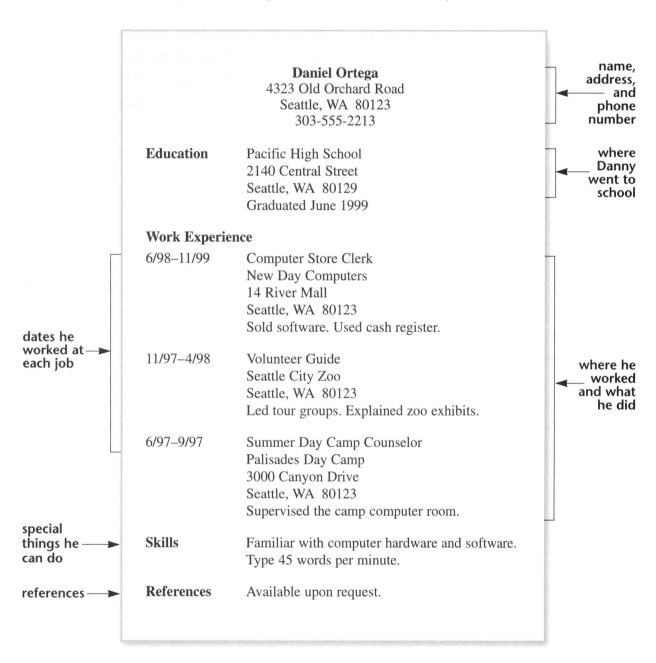

Daniel Ortega
4323 Old Orchard Road
Seattle, WA 80123
303-555-2213

Education	Pacific High School 2140 Central Street Seattle, WA 80129 Graduated June 1999

Work Experience

6/98–11/99	Computer Store Clerk New Day Computers 14 River Mall Seattle, WA 80123 Sold software. Used cash register.
11/97–4/98	Volunteer Guide Seattle City Zoo Seattle, WA 80123 Led tour groups. Explained zoo exhibits.
6/97–9/97	Summer Day Camp Counselor Palisades Day Camp 3000 Canyon Drive Seattle, WA 80123 Supervised the camp computer room.
Skills	Familiar with computer hardware and software. Type 45 words per minute.
References	Available upon request.

name, address, and phone number

where Danny went to school

dates he worked at each job

where he worked and what he did

special things he can do

references

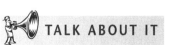

TALK ABOUT IT When did Danny work at a computer store? When did he graduate from high school? What other information did Danny give in his résumé?

TRY IT

Danny gets a job at Computer Zone. That is a store at 333 Waldorf Road, Seattle, Washington 80138. Danny works there from February 2000 (2/00) to December 2000 (12/00). He sells computer hardware.

Danny studies computer programming at Allied Technical School. The courses run from September 2000 (9/00) to June 2001 (6/01). The school's address is 5400 Central Avenue in Burnside, Washington 81230.

Danny needs to update his résumé. He decides to include only his computer store jobs. Add the facts above to the résumé.

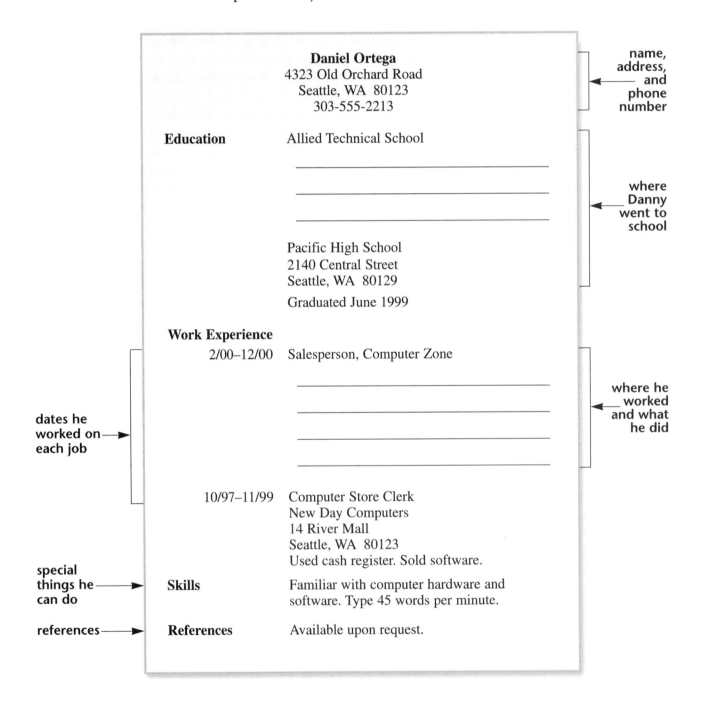

Use the Checklist to see if you have filled out Danny's résumé completely.

✔ Checklist

Does the new résumé include:

❑ Danny's name, address, and phone number at the top?

❑ categories on the left?

❑ the names and addresses of Danny's schools?

❑ Danny's most recent education listed first?

❑ Danny's most recent job listed first?

❑ Danny's other jobs and skills?

Are there any changes you forgot to make on the résumé? If so, go back and make them now.

USE IT

Now write a résumé for yourself. Use Danny Ortega's résumé as a guide. First center your full name, address, and phone number at the top of the page. Then list details and dates about your own education and jobs. Think of two people to use as references. List their names on the résumé, or type *Available upon request.*

Prepare a draft of your résumé on a separate sheet of paper. Use the space below to make notes to help you organize your thoughts.

Reminder

Résumés should always be carefully typed.

Use the Checklist to make sure your résumé is complete. Now type your résumé on another sheet of paper. Make sure you proofread it carefully! Save your résumé in your portfolio.

Lesson 2 Letters of Application

Learning Objective
To ask about a job by writing a letter of application

Words to Know
letter of application a business letter to an employer asking about a job

 LEARN IT

To get a job, you may need to write a letter. You may see a classified ad in the newspaper. The ad may ask interested workers to write for details. Or you may already know where you want to work. You might send a **letter of application** there to ask about a job.

In the first paragraph of your letter, ask about a specific job. If you saw a classified ad, give the name of the job. Also give the name and date of the newspaper.

Next, tell the employer about your good points. You can also "sell" yourself a little. Tell why you would be right for this job.

Finally, ask the employer for an interview. In an interview, you will talk to the employer. It is the next step in getting the job.

A letter of application is a business letter. You can use either the modified-block or full-block style. You should type the letter if possible. Be polite, but not too personal. Do not write a long letter. An interested employer can find out more about you in an interview.

Reminder

The six parts of a business letter are heading, inside address, greeting, body, closing, and signature.

A letter of application should include:

- the six parts of a business letter
- the name of a specific job that interests you
- the reasons you are the right person for the job
- a request for an interview

When might you write a letter of application? What kind of job might you like to apply for someday?

 **LOOK AT IT**

Danny Ortega sees a classified ad in the newspaper. A computer company needs an assistant. Danny thinks the job is right for him. The ad asks people to write to Mr. Thomas Peters at Computer Networks.

Danny writes a letter of application. He uses Mr. Peters's name and address in the inside address. His letter of application is typed in full-block style.

heading →

inside address →

greeting →

body:
- what job Danny wants
- why he is the right person for the job
- ask for an interview

closing →

signature →

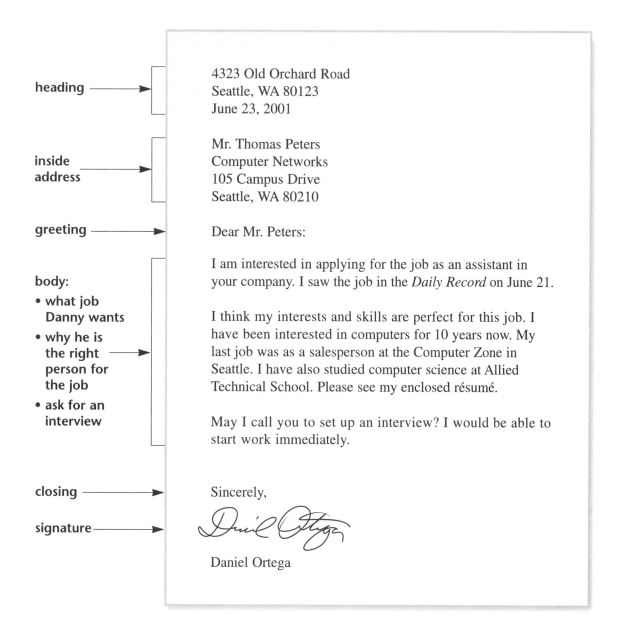

4323 Old Orchard Road
Seattle, WA 80123
June 23, 2001

Mr. Thomas Peters
Computer Networks
105 Campus Drive
Seattle, WA 80210

Dear Mr. Peters:

I am interested in applying for the job as an assistant in your company. I saw the job in the *Daily Record* on June 21.

I think my interests and skills are perfect for this job. I have been interested in computers for 10 years now. My last job was as a salesperson at the Computer Zone in Seattle. I have also studied computer science at Allied Technical School. Please see my enclosed résumé.

May I call you to set up an interview? I would be able to start work immediately.

Sincerely,

Daniel Ortega

 **TALK ABOUT IT**

How does Danny suggest that he is right for the job? What request does Danny make in his letter?

 **TRY IT**

Danny does not get an interview with Mr. Peters. On June 28, Danny sees an ad in the *Observer.* Camp Howell, a computer camp for children, needs a senior counselor. The counselor should be experienced with computers. He should enjoy working with children. The job runs from July 7 to August 28. Danny once worked at a camp, and he thinks he might enjoy this job.

Camp Howell is at 1120 Overlook Drive, Seattle, Washington 80010. The director is Kristen Lo. Write Danny's letter of application to Ms. Lo.

heading ———▶

4323 Old Orchard Road

_____

_____

June 29, 2001

inside address ———▶

Ms. Kristen Lo
Camp Howell

_____

_____

greeting ———▶

_____:

body:
• **what job Danny wants**
• **why he is the right person for the job**
• **ask for an interview**

———▶

I am interested in applying for the job of senior counselor at Camp Howell.

_____

_____

_____

_____

_____

closing ———▶

_____

signature ———▶

Daniel Ortega

Use the Checklist to make sure your letter of application is complete.

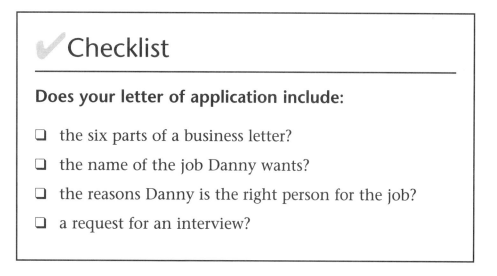

✔ Checklist

Does your letter of application include:

❑ the six parts of a business letter?

❑ the name of the job Danny wants?

❑ the reasons Danny is the right person for the job?

❑ a request for an interview?

Is your letter of application clear and complete? If not, go back and work on it some more.

 USE IT Write a letter of application for a job. It could be for a part-time job or a summer job. You might find this job listed in the classified ads of your local newspaper. Or you might know a place where you would like to work.

Follow the steps in this lesson as you write. Make notes for your letter in the space below. Then prepare a draft on a separate sheet of paper. You can use either the modified-block or full-block style.

Use the Checklist to make sure your letter is complete. Now write or type your letter of application on a separate sheet of paper. Remember to check your spelling and punctuation carefully. Save your letter in your portfolio.

Lesson 3 | Job Application Forms

Learning Objective

To apply for a job by filling out an application

Words to Know

job application a form with questions you must answer when you apply for a job

 LEARN IT

Filling out a **job application**, or application for employment, is part of looking for a job. The application form will ask where and when you went to school. It will ask about other jobs you have had. The answers to these questions should be on your résumé. If you carry a résumé with you, you will have these details handy.

Applications are important. Employers will look at your application and then decide if they want to meet you. Print neatly in ink. Take care with spelling. Make sure you understand each question before you answer it. Fill in all the blanks. If a question does not apply to you, write *N/A*. That means the question does "not apply." Ask for a second application if you need one. Then copy your answers neatly.

The application will ask personal questions. It may ask if you are a citizen. It may ask about health problems. Give honest answers to all questions. Most employers check your answers. At the same time, show your best self. List any training or skills that might help you get the job.

A job application should include:

- details about your education and work history
- correct answers to all questions
- all answers printed neatly in ink

Why should a job application be neat and complete?

 **LOOK AT IT**   Camp Howell asks Danny Ortega to come in for an interview. While he is there, he fills out the application form below. He decides to only list his computer jobs.

Camp Howell — Application for Employment

personal information →

Name *(last)* Ortega   *(first)* Daniel

Address 4323 Old Orchard Road

Seattle, WA 80123   Home phone (303) 555–2213

Social Security Number 127 - 74 - 0713   Date of birth July 1, 1981

Position desired Senior Counselor   Date you can start Immediately

Are you employed now? No   If so, may we speak to your present employer? N/A

Do you have health problems that may interfere with your work? No   If yes, explain:

_____

schools Danny has attended →

Education

Circle last year completed.   Describe any other training or education.

Middle School   6   7   ⑧   Allied Technical School

High School   1   2   3   ④   Courses in Computer Programming

College   1   2   3   4   _____

jobs he has had →

Work History

Name of Company	Dates Worked	Position
Computer Zone	2/00–12/00	Salesperson
New Day Computer Store	6/98–11/99	Salesperson
Palisades Day Camp	6/97–9/97	Camp Computer Counselor

people who know him well →

References

Name	Phone Number
1. Dr. Donald Min	(303) 555–2189
2. Mrs. Helen Peters	(303) 555–7892
3. _____	(___) _____

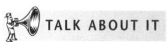 **TALK ABOUT IT**   What experience does Danny have with computers? What experience does he have as a camp counselor? Who are his references?

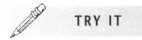 **TRY IT**

Danny did not get the job at Camp Howell. On July 20, 2001, he applies for a job as a repairperson at Computers Unlimited. The company helps businesses solve computer problems. He can start on August 1. He asks for $350 a week. He has never applied to this company before. After an interview, Danny gets the job!

Fill in Danny's application. Use the information above. Also use details from Danny's résumé and application on pages 177 and 185.

COMPUTERS *unlimited*

Application for Employment

	DATE

Personal Information

personal information →

NAME   Daniel Ortega

ADDRESS

HOME PHONE

SOCIAL SECURITY NUMBER	DATE OF BIRTH

Employment Desired

job that he wants →

POSITION DESIRED **Repairperson**	DATE YOU CAN START

SALARY DESIRED

ARE YOU EMPLOYED NOW?   **no**

IF SO, MAY WE TALK TO YOUR PRESENT EMPLOYER?

HAVE YOU EVER APPLIED TO THIS COMPANY BEFORE?

IF SO, WHEN?

Education

schools he has attended →

	SCHOOL	YEARS ATTENDED	DATE GRADUATED
HIGH SCHOOL	**Pacific High School**		**June 1999**
COLLEGE OR TECHNICAL SCHOOL			

Work History

jobs he has had →

NAME OF COMPANY	TYPE OF WORK	DATES

References

people who know him well →

NAME	POSITION	TELEPHONE

Use the Checklist to see if the application form is complete.

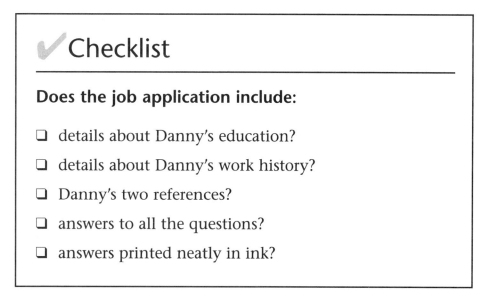

✔ Checklist

Does the job application include:

❑ details about Danny's education?

❑ details about Danny's work history?

❑ Danny's two references?

❑ answers to all the questions?

❑ answers printed neatly in ink?

Is the job application form complete? If not, go back and add details that could help Danny get the job.

USE IT

Reminder

When you fill out a real job application, be sure to ask people before you use their name as a reference.

Imagine you are applying for a job. Look at the Job Application Form, which is Form 16A in *Forms in the Real World*. You can make notes in the space below to help you organize your thoughts. Use facts about yourself. Include details about your own education and work history. For references, choose two people who would speak highly of you.

Use the Checklist to make sure your information is complete. Now fill in the job application form. Save the completed form in your portfolio.

Lesson 4 W-4 Forms

Learning Objective

To begin paying taxes on your salary by filling out a W-4 form

Words to Know

W-4 form a federal tax form

LEARN IT

When you get a job, you must fill out a **W-4 form**. This form asks you to claim dependents, or people you support. If you are not married and have no children, you have only one dependent—yourself. Employers use your W-4 form to figure out how much tax to take out of your paycheck. Fill out the W-4 form honestly.

A W-4 form should include:

- your name, address, and Social Security number

- a check mark that shows if you are married or single

- how many dependents you have

LOOK AT IT   When Danny Ortega gets a job, he fills out this W-4 form.

name   address   married or single?   Social Security number

Form **W-4**	Employee's Withholding Allowance Certificate	OMB No. 1545-0010
Department of the Treasury Internal Revenue Service	▶ For Privacy Act and Paperwork Reduction Act Notice, see page 2.	2001

1 Type or print your first name and middle initial	Last name	2 Your Social Security number
Daniel A.	Ortega	127 74 0713

Home address (number and street or rural route)
4323 Old Orchard Rd.

3 ☒ Single ☐ Married ☐ Married, but withhold at higher Single rate.
Note: If married, but legally separated, or spouse is a nonresident alien, check the Single box.

City or town, state, and ZIP code
Seattle, WA 80123

4   If your last name differs from that on your social security card, check here. **You** must call 1-800-772-1213 for a new card . . . . ▶ ☐

5   Total number of allowances you are claiming (from line H above or from the worksheets on page 2 if they apply) . .   **5** 1

6   Additional amount, if any, you want withheld from each paycheck . . . .   **6** $

7   I claim exemption from withholding for 2000, and I certify that I meet **BOTH** of the following conditions for exemption:
  • Last year I had a right to a refund of **ALL** Federal income tax withheld because I had **NO** tax liability **AND**
  • This year I expect a refund of **ALL** Federal income tax withheld because I expect to have **NO** tax liability.
  If you meet both conditions, write EXEMPT here . . . . . . ▶   **7**

Under penalties of perjury, I certify that I am entitled to the number of withholding allowances claimed on this certificate, or I am entitled to claim exempt status.
Employee's signature
(Form is not valid unless you sign it) ▶

◀ signature   How many people do you support?

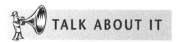 **TALK ABOUT IT** Is Danny married? Does he have children? How do you know?

 **TRY IT**

On the same day Danny gets his job, the company also hires Danielle Greene. Danielle is single and has two children. She lives at 2456 Evergreen Circle, Seattle, Washington 80101. Her Social Security number is 112-56-8976. Danielle claims three dependents on line 5.

Fill in the W-4 form for Danielle Greene.

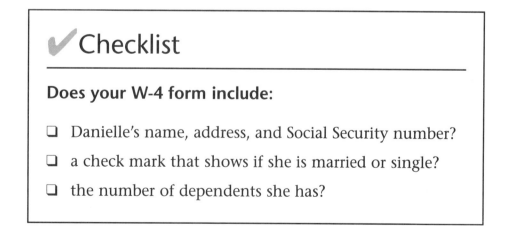

Use the Checklist to make sure the W-4 form is complete.

✔ Checklist

Does your W-4 form include:

❑ Danielle's name, address, and Social Security number?

❑ a check mark that shows if she is married or single?

❑ the number of dependents she has?

 USE IT Now use your own information to fill in Form 17A in *Forms in the Real World.* Use the Checklist to make sure your form is complete. Save your W-4 Form in your portfolio.

Chapter 3

Apply It in the Real World

Searching for a New Job

Danny Ortega worked at Computers Limited for one year. Then the company closed. Now Danny wants to work at Midtown Computers. Midtown has the biggest repair shop in Seattle. Its address is 7675 Broadway, Seattle, Washington 80236.

Here are the things that Danny has to do:

1. A sign in Midtown's window says the company needs a repairperson. Danny wants to get an interview with Ms. Walker, the director of the repair division.

2. Danny must add his work at Computers Limited to his résumé. This will show Midtown that he has experience repairing computers.

3. Sam Smith, Danny's boss at Computers Limited, trained Danny to do many different kinds of repairs. Danny now wants to be a senior repairperson. He wants to earn $400 a week. Mr. Smith said that Danny could use him as a reference. Mr. Smith's phone number is 303-555-1332.

4. Midtown hired Danny as a senior repairperson. Now he has to fill out a tax form from the government. He still claims only himself as a dependent.

Decide and Write

A. In a small group, talk about each situation above. What kind of writing might Danny need for each one?

B. Now have each student in your group fill out one of the forms in *Forms in the Real World* or write or type a response. You may need to look at the lessons in this chapter for addresses or other details. Save your work in your portfolio.

WRAP-UP

In Unit Five, you learned about the kinds of writing people do at work. In Chapter 1, you practiced types of writing people do in offices. In Chapter 2, you wrote different kinds of business letters. In Chapter 3, you practiced types of writing you can do to find a job.

WRITING at WORK

Learning Basic Job Skills	Working with Other Businesses	Looking for Jobs
• Telephone Messages	• Purchase Order Forms	• Résumés
• Memos	• Letters of Request	• Letters of Application
• Fax Cover Sheets	• Letters of Complaint	• Job Application Forms
• E-mail Messages	• Follow-up Letters	• W-4 Forms

Read the types of writing on the chart. Then choose two types of writing. On the lines below, describe a time in your own life when you may be able to use each type of writing.

1. _____

_____

2. _____

_____

What Did You Learn?

On page 138, you listed ways in which writing might be useful in a job. Look again at this list. Can you think of more types of writing to add to the list? What forms might you add?

Some Useful Abbreviations

POSTAL ABBREVIATIONS FOR U.S. STATES

Alabama	AL	Montana	MT
Alaska	AK	Nebraska	NE
Arizona	AZ	Nevada	NV
Arkansas	AR	New Hampshire	NH
California	CA	New Jersey	NJ
Colorado	CO	New Mexico	NM
Connecticut	CT	New York	NY
Delaware	DE	North Carolina	NC
District of Columbia	DC	North Dakota	ND
Florida	FL	Ohio	OH
Georgia	GA	Oklahoma	OK
Hawaii	HI	Oregon	OR
Idaho	ID	Pennsylvania	PA
Illinois	IL	Puerto Rico	PR
Indiana	IN	Rhode Island	RI
Iowa	IA	South Carolina	SC
Kansas	KS	South Dakota	SD
Kentucky	KY	Tennessee	TN
Louisiana	LA	Texas	TX
Maine	ME	Utah	UT
Maryland	MD	Vermont	VT
Massachusetts	MA	Virginia	VA
Michigan	MI	Washington (state)	WA
Minnesota	MN	West Virginia	WV
Mississippi	MS	Wisconsin	WI
Missouri	MO	Wyoming	WY

ADDRESS ABBREVIATIONS

Avenue	Ave.
Boulevard	Blvd.
Court	Ct.
Drive	Dr.
East	E.
Heights	Hts.
Highway	Hwy.
Lane	Ln.
North	N.
Parkway	Pky.
Place	Pl.
Road	Rd.
South	S.
Square	Sq.
Street	St.
Terrace	Ter.
Turnpike	Tpke.
West	W.

ABBREVIATIONS ON FORMS

ACCT.	account
N/A	Not Applicable
APT.	apartment
NO. or #	number
D.O.B.	date of birth
SOC. SEC.#	Social Security number
EXT.	extension (of a telephone number)
P.O. BOX	post office box
M.I.	middle initial
TEL. NO.	telephone number
MO.	month
YR.	year